Editor-in-Chief and Founder:
 *Lyndon H. LaRouche, Jr.*
Editorial Board: *Lyndon H. LaRouche, Jr. , Helga
 Zepp-LaRouche, Robert Ingraham, Tony
 Papert, Gerald Rose, Dennis Small, Jeffrey
 Steinberg, William Wertz*
Co-Editors: *Robert Ingraham, Tony Papert*
Managing Editor: *Nancy Spannaus*
Technology: *Marsha Freeman*
Books: *Katherine Notley*
Ebooks: *Richard Burden*
Graphics: *Alan Yue*
Photos: *Stuart Lewis*
Circulation Manager: *Stanley Ezrol*

INTELLIGENCE DIRECTORS
Counterintelligence: *Jeffrey Steinberg, Michele
 Steinberg*
Economics: *John Hoefle, Marcia Merry Baker,
 Paul Gallagher*
History: *Anton Chaitkin*
Ibero-America: *Dennis Small*
Russia and Eastern Europe: *Rachel Douglas*
United States: *Debra Freeman*

INTERNATIONAL BUREAUS
Bogotá: *Miriam Redondo*
Berlin: *Rainer Apel*
Copenhagen: *Tom Gillesberg*
Houston: *Harley Schlanger*
Lima: *Sara Madueño*
Melbourne: *Robert Barwick*
Mexico City: *Gerardo Castilleja Chávez*
New Delhi: *Ramtanu Maitra*
Paris: *Christine Bierre*
Stockholm: *Ulf Sandmark*
United Nations, N.Y.C.: *Leni Rubinstein*
Washington, D.C.: *William Jones*
Wiesbaden: *Göran Haglund*

ON THE WEB
e-mail: eirns@larouchepub.com
www.larouchepub.com
www.executiveintelligencereview.com
www.larouchepub.com/eiw
Webmaster: *John Sigerson*
Assistant Webmaster: *George Hollis*
Editor, Arabic-language edition: *Hussein Askary*

EIR (ISSN 0273-6314) *is published weekly
(50 issues), by EIR News Service, Inc.,
P.O. Box 17390, Washington, D.C. 20041-0390.
(703) 777-9451 ext. 415*

**European Headquarters:** E.I.R. GmbH, Postfach
Bahnstrasse 9a, D-65205, Wiesbaden, Germany
Tel: 49-611-73650
Homepage: http://www.eirna.com
e-mail: eirna@eirna.com
Director: Georg Neudecker

**Montreal, Canada:** 514-461-1557

**Denmark:** EIR - Danmark, Sankt Knuds Vej 11,
basement left, DK-1903 Frederiksberg, Denmark.
Tel.: +45 35 43 60 40, Fax: +45 35 43 87 57. e-mail:
eirdk@hotmail.com.

**Mexico City:** EIR, Sor Juana Inés de la Cruz 242-2
Col. Agricultura C.P. 11360
Delegación M. Hidalgo, México D.F.
Tel. (5525) 5318-2301
eirmexico@gmail.com

Canada Post Publication Sales Agreement
#40683579

**Postmaster:** Send all address changes to *EIR*, P.O.
Box 17390, Washington, D.C. 20041-0390.

Signed articles in *EIR* represent the views of the
authors, and not necessarily those of the Editorial
Board.

# Jail Obama for Treason!

# Jail Obama for Treason!

Feb. 20—Barack Obama, after eight years of mass killing with drones and genocidal "regime change" wars, has refused to retire from his treasonous role, but is now leading an insurrection against the democratically elected President who solidly defeated his clone, Hillary Clinton, in the November election.

"Obama is actually highly vulnerable," Lyndon LaRouche noted today. "He has exposed himself as a traitor to the United States."

Obama proudly met with his CIA chief John Brennan every Tuesday afternoon during his reign to draw up the "kill list" for the week—those whom "King Obama" chose to assassinate on his own volition—*sans* court order, *sans* due process—along with whoever happened to be with his target when the drone struck.

LaRouche noted that the *New York Times* long ago revealed the story of Obama's Tuesday kill-list sessions, not because they wanted to expose his killer character, but to drive the U.S. population to accept it—to belittle themselves by tolerating a mass killer as their president, without protest.

*EIR* is releasing a dossier this week entitled "Obama and Soros—Nazis in Ukraine 2014—U.S. in 2017?" Feb. 21-22 is the third anniversary of Obama's overthrow of the democratically elected government of Ukraine in 2014, in a violent mob action directly funded and directed by Obama and his personal agent to the region, Victoria Nuland. The riots, centered in the Maidan central square, featured molotov-cocktail attacks on police and government buildings, led by organizations openly promoting Stepan Bandera, Adolph Hitler's Ukrainian nazi partner.

The *EIR* dossier demonstrates that Barack Obama, with his sponsor George Soros and other British and U.S. "project democracy" agents, are now turning their "color revolution" fire on the United States itself—and for the same reason: the British Empire refused to allow Western Europe and Russia to work together for peace and development, and therefore ran an anti-Russia coup by old-line nazis in Ukraine, to refuel the old nazi hatred of Russia.

So also in the Uunited States: the Obama gang is making the incredibly pathetic effort to convince Americans that President Trump has committed a crime by wanting to *prevent* a war with Russia, and to instead work with Russia—and China and India and Japan—to bring peace and development to the world, including to the United States.

While there are dupes in the United States who will swallow such garbage, the majority of the population is in a state of revolt against such psychotic nonsense, be it from the politicians or from the media.

Obama and Hillary Clinton had brought the world to the very edge of thermonuclear war with Russia. That danger has been dramatically curtailed by Hillary's defeat. And yet, the Obama/Soros gang is calling for the impeachment or criminal prosecution of Trump, who is making peace with Russia. The Obama/Soros gang claims instead that it is dangerous for Trump to have "his finger on the nuclear button"!

To bring this ugly irony to an end, requires that Obama be brought to justice. His multiple crimes as president are now compounded by his overt campaign to overthrow the government of the United States of America—an overt act of treason.

Obama so loved the British Queen and the British system, that he served as its loyal asset in restoring the subservience of the former British colony to the British System—by monetarism and colonial wars. Today, the *Financial Times*, the voice of the London and Wall Street financial oligarchy, calls openly for a violent insurrection against the upstart President, who is threatening to end the British Empire's "divide and conquer" division of the world. The *FT* bureau chief in Washington, Edward Luce, warns that if Trump is not taken down, he will take down "the system."

Indeed he might, and so be it. Trump has argued that the United States accept the proposals from Putin—that we work hand in hand to defeat terrorism—and from Xi Jinping to join the New Silk Road process for global development. For Trump to live up to that commitment would mean the end of Empire. It is the responsibility of an inspired population to bring about that beautiful result, and that inspiration is best expressed by the fifty years of leadership from Lyndon LaRouche. This is our moment, if we take it, to bring about what Helga Zepp-LaRouche has called the "adulthood" of humanity.

# EIR Contents

www.larouchepub.com Volume 44, Number 8, February 24, 2017

*Cover This Week*

*Color revolution in Ukraine. Maidan Square, Kiev, February 18, 2014.*

Creative Commons

# I. Obama and Soros— Nazis in Ukraine 2014—U.S. in 2017?

# How Obama and Soros Put Actual Nazis in Power in Ukraine

## INTRODUCTION

Feb 20—Three years ago this week, a Molotov-cocktail-throwing mob on the streets of Kiev occupied government buildings, perpetrating violence and driving the duly elected president of the nation out of office and out of the country. The leading groups in the mob were waving portraits of Stepan Bandera, Adolf Hitler's collaborator in Ukraine during World War II.

Today, the same British and American intelligence institutions, and many of the same individuals, are attempting to repeat the process, only this time the target is the democratically elected government of the United States itself. The reasoning is the same: the Empire must maintain the division of the world into competing blocs, the divide and conquer policy of Empire since the time of the Romans. The East vs. West divide nearly collapsed when the Soviet Union collapsed in the 1990s, ending the excuse of the Free World vs. Godless Communism which had been used by the British to break up Franklin Roosevelt's partnership with Russia to defeat fascism.

Lyndon and Helga LaRouche, at the time of the Soviet collapse, offered the idea of a New Silk Road, uniting Europe with Asia via new, high-speed rail development corridors through Russia and Central Asia, to unite the world on the basis of mutual development and cultural dialogue. This the Empire would not allow.

The Obama Administration, and London, not only welcomed the violent coup in Ukraine in 2014, as a means to justify a new NATO military mobilization against Russia, but rather, they created it. Obama and his spokesmen proudly announced that the United States had financed and orchestrated the organizations participating in the demonstrations on the public square, the Maidan. Obama's direct agent for the coup, Assistant Secretary of State for European and Eurasian Affairs, Victoria Nuland, visited the rioters several times, handing out cookies on the Maidan, while refusing to acknowledge that in addition to peaceful demonstrators concerned about corruption and economic hardships, there were also openly neo-fascist gangs conducting an armed insurrection against the elected government.

Nuland was also caught by a phone tap instructing the U.S. Ambassador to Ukraine on precisely who was to be made Prime Minister in the new government, after the President was toppled.

The result of the coup for the Ukrainian people has been an unmitigated horror. The prosperity promised in

Wikimedia Commons

*The youth group of the Social-National Party of Ukraine, on the march with their swastika banner in Lviv in 1999. The swastika was dropped in 2003 and the party was renamed Svoboda in 2004.*

exchange for signing a free-trade Association Agreement with the European Union (EU), has not materialized; instead there has been vicious austerity, massive budget cutting, and lay-offs, while foreign nationals were appointed to run the economy. Government military forces and neo-Nazi militias carry out perpetual warfare against the Donbass region of the country, which refused to submit to the illegal coup.

The myth was peddled in the West that Russia caused the problem, by objecting to the peaceful uprising against their puppet government in Kiev, then annexing Crimea and invading the Donbass, while plotting to conquer Ukraine, the Baltic countries, and perhaps others, intent on restoring the Soviet Empire.

So also today, the myth is spread by the defeated Obama and George Soros circles, and *ad nauseam* in the mainstream press, that the Obama/Hillary campaign was only defeated because Russia stole the election, in order to have their puppet Donald Trump win the election. Without ever offering a shred of evidence (it is all top secret, don't you know), mass hysteria against Putin and Russia is fueled by leaks from the same neoconservative intelligence networks left over from the Obama administration. Trump has identified these criminals, naming elements in the FBI and the NSA, and only stopped short of identifying their actions as treasonous. The President is correct.

Putin himself has been very clear about what is going on in the United States. Asked at a press conference on Jan. 17 about the anti-Russian hysteria in the U.S. press and in some political circles, Putin said:

In my opinion, there are several goals; some are obvious. The first is to undermine the legitimacy of the elected president of the United States. Incidentally, in this connection I would like to note that whether people who do it want it or not, they greatly damage U.S. interests. It seems that they trained for this in Kiev, and now are ready to organize a Maidan in Washington not to let Trump assume office. The second goal is to tie the hands and legs of the newly-elected president related to the implementation of his pre-election campaign promises to the American people and the international community.

Meanwhile, in Ukraine, Dr. Natalia Vitrenko, the

*Natalia Vitrenko, doctor of economics, is chairman of the Progressive Socialist Party of Ukraine, has served in Parliament, and has run for President.*

presidential candidate for the Progressive Socialist Party of Ukraine in several elections, in a letter to President Trump after his election, called on him to change the disastrous Obama policy regarding Ukraine:

Our people are suffering badly from war, extreme poverty, corruption, political repressions, and the rampaging of neo-Nazis. The outgoing U.S. Administration kept stirring up the people of Ukraine against Russia, thereby inciting a war between our fraternal peoples, one that unquestionably threatens to trigger a Third World War.

The fascist elements in the Ukraine government have orchestrated thug attacks against Vitrenko and her party, seized the party headquarters, and are threatening to bring charges against her for treason for the "crime" of identifying the openly fascist actions of the government and the neo-Nazi militias.

And in the United States, Obama is the first president in U.S. history to lead an effort to bring down the government that replaced him. Under Obama, the United States conducted perpetual warfare against countries which were no threat to our nation, conducted drone strikes against individuals personally chosen by Obama without even a semblance of due process, and nearly provoked a war with Russia, a war which would almost certainly have been thermonuclear, and which would have been nearly certain if Obama's clone, Hillary Clinton, had been elected.

The idea that Trump may end the imperial policy, and join forces with Russia and China, as Franklin Roosevelt did to defeat fascism, in the new paradigm of defeating terrorism, and building infrastructure and agro-industrial advancement for nations throughout the world as part of the New Silk Road process, would mean the end of the very concept of Empire, once and for all. To prevent this, the British and their assets in the United States, led by Obama and his sponsor George Soros as well as their fellow neocons on the Republican side, will stop at nothing. The American people are increasingly aware of this evil, but must move quickly to expose it and crush it.

This report is divided into five sections, with links to documentation articles at the end.

1. The strategic situation in Ukraine, from the February 2014 neo-Nazi coup through the collapse of that nation into economic and strategic chaos today.

2. The neo-Nazi provenance of the leading groups and individuals in the 2014 regime-change coup in Ukraine.

3. A chronology of the coup itself, from November 2013 through February 2014.

4. A profile of the origins and methods of the color revolution policy, deployed against Ukraine in the coup, and in the United States today.

5. The appeal by Dr. Natalia Vitrenko, presidential candidate for the Progressive Socialist Party of Ukraine, to the EU on Feb. 10, 2017, to stop the repression by the Kiev government.

The potential for the world to leave the era of imperial control behind, to enter a new era of civilization just as the Renaissance ended the era of feudal backwardness, is within our grasp today. It is up to each and every citizen of the United States, and citizens of the world, to make this moment of huge potential become a reality.

# Anglo-American War Party Seeks To Blow Up Ukraine, Wreck U.S.-Russian Prospects

Feb. 20—Three years ago, on Feb. 22, 2014, the prolonged, increasingly violent Euromaidan *coup d'état* was completed in Ukraine against the country's elected President Victor Yanukovych. His life in peril as commandoes from the so-called Maidan Self-Defense Forces threatened to storm his residence at dawn if he didn't quit, yet unwilling to use military force to crush the thousands of demonstrators still in the Maidan (Independence Square) in downtown Kiev, Yanukovych fled the capital. Unable to regroup in the northeastern city of Kharkov or his native Donetsk, he ultimately sought asylum in Russia.

The coup of November 2013-February 2014 was built on the precedent of Ukraine's 2004 Orange Revolution, when Yanukovych's first election had been challenged as fraudulent by a Maidan demonstration, on the color revolution model of Anglo-American financier George Soros and the American professional organizer Gene Sharp. The demonstrators in December 2004 forced a revote, which Yanukovych lost. Within months, the victorious Orange revolutionaries were squabbling over power, as the Ukrainian economy continued to dive under their deregulation and privatization policies, and

kowtowing to the austerity demands of the International Monetary Fund. Yanukovych ran again in 2010 and won.

But the more than 2000 non-governmental organizations (NGOs) in Ukraine, funded by the U.S. government, the UK, the EU, and Soros's private Open Society projects, continued to shape public opinion in Ukraine after the Orange Revolution. U.S. Assistant Secretary of State Victoria Nuland boasted that US$5 billion had gone into Ukraine through State Department channels alone, much of it, as the Ukrainian-born Russian economist Sergei Glazyev put it, issued in the form of grants to develop an intellectual community of experts, oriented against the Russian Federation and directed toward shaping Russophobic attitudes in Ukrainian society.

The new dimension in the Euromaidan, one that was pre-planned, was violent provocations and ultimately a violent overthrow of the government. Yanukovych's November 2013 decision to delay signing an Association Agreement with the European Union, after he realized that it would damage Ukraine's economy, was taken as the pretext for a full-scale coup. The Maidan organizers poured into central Kiev and announced

*Neo-Nazi protestors in the Maidan, January 2014.*

they would not leave until the decision was rescinded and Yanukovych left office.

While many people came to the Maidan waving EU flags and were full of hope for a better life, the paramilitary groups, who repeatedly escalated the violence and sabotaged every interim agreement to resolve the standoff, marched under the red and black flag of the Organization of Ukrainian Nationalists (OUN), the mid-20th-century fascist movement of Stepan Bandera. The OUN had collaborated with the Nazis during World War II and carried out the ethnic-cleansing mass murder of Poles and Jews on its own, as well. These neo-Nazi groups called themselves Right Sector; their formation and build-up during 1991-2013 stemmed directly out of funding to Bandera's followers by MI6 and the Allen Dulles wing of the American CIA during the Cold War.

It was the coup-installed regime's immediate move to demote the Russian language, which is spoken throughout much of Ukraine, from its status as a second official language, and a series of attacks by Right Sector in Crimea and the eastern industrial region called the Donbass, that set off a momentous cascade of events in 2014. By mid-March, Crimea had seceded from Ukraine and voted to join the Russian Federation. In the Donbass, the autonomous Donetsk Peoples Republic (DPR) and Lugansk Peoples Republic (LPR) were declared, rejecting the Kiev coup and laying claim to the major cities and much of the territory of those two districts. At least ten thousand people have died in the ensuing civil war, as Kiev sent army units and Right Sector-based battalions into the Donbass to attempt to quell the Donbass militias' uprising.

**Unfrozen conflict**

In February 2015, negotiations held in the capital of Belarus and conducted by the leaders of France, Germany, Russia, and Ukraine, reached the Minsk II agreement between Kiev and the Donbass republics, for a ceasefire and prospective political settlement in that region. Heavy weaponry began to be pulled back from the line of contact between their respective military forces.

The ceasefire has been overseen and monitored, since then, by the Organization for Security and Cooperation in Europe (OSCE), an East-West club dating back to the 1970s. Disagreements remained over the meaning of the Minsk II commitment to Constitutional changes in Ukraine, allowing extreme autonomy for the DPR and LPR. To date, the radical nationalists in the Ukrainian Parliament, with Right Sector figures among them, have refused to make such revisions. Nonetheless, the fighting and huge civilian loss of life had abated over the past two years, as if the Donbass were becoming one of ECE's notorious frozen conflicts.

In December 2016, as President-elect Donald Trump continued to signal his wish for normalizing relations with Russia, the Donbass began to heat up again. The initiative came from the Kiev side. Even pro-Maidan analysts reported, as the *Kyiv Post* did on Jan. 26, that Ukrainian forces have staged what has become known as a creeping offensive to regain control over territory in the gray zone, the no-man's land that divides separatist and government forces in the eastern regions of Donetsk and Lugansk.

Analysts at Radio Free Europe/Radio Liberty, a U.S. Government-funded outlet, acknowledged that pro-Kiev troops have sparked bloody clashes with the Donbass forces. Alexander Hug, deputy chief of the OSCE's Special Monitoring Mission for Ukraine, reported that Kiev's forces had positioned large-caliber artillery including towed howitzers, main battle tanks, and multiple-launch rocket systems banned under the Minsk deal in the open with impunity.

With the neo-Nazi Right Sector and its offshoot battalions, it is never easy to say exactly who has provided the impetus for their actions. But a look around London and Washington quickly turns up who is cheering them on.

U.S. war party Senators John McCain and Lindsey Graham (Republicans), along with Obama-ite Democratic Senator Amy Klobuchar, spent New Year's Eve with Kiev troops near the front line with the DPR. They also toured the Baltic countries, where NATO's latest military build-up is under way. On Feb. 2, McCain issued a letter to President Trump, ignoring the OSCE report, and blaming the Donbass escalation on Russia and its proxy forces, demanding that the U.S.A. supply Kiev with "defensive lethal assistance" weapons.

Ukraine President Petro Poroshenko, on Feb. 1, launched a round of grandstanding about his intention to hold a referendum in Ukraine on joining NATO. Prime Minister Volodymyr Hroysman visited NATO Headquarters in Brussels on Feb. 9, to meet with NATO Deputy Secretary General Rose Gottemoeller, formerly an under secretary of state in the Obama Administration.

Atlanticist think-tankers chimed in, with a barrage of publications "warning" that Trump will make a deal over Ukraine: James Sherr of Chatham House in the UK sounded an alarm against pre-emptive compromise over Ukraine; Russian anti-Putin analyst Pavel Felgenhauer, writing for the neoconservative Jamestown Foundation's *Eurasia Daily Monitor,* wailed, "If Trump hands over Ukraine, he will make Russia great again;" Adrian Karatnycky of the Atlantic Council pre-emptively accused Trump of preparing to sell out Ukraine by lifting sanctions on Russia while, so he claimed, Russian-backed forces started a brutal offensive within Ukraine.

Russian Foreign Minister Sergei Lavrov devoted nearly half of his Feb. 12 Sunday prime time interview on Russia's NTV channel to a measured discussion of Ukraine. Speaking of the recent escalation, Lavrov said, "The only advantage I see in this situation, which we arrived at with much bloodshed and after many months, even years of experiments, is that the West is finally beginning to understand what the Ukrainian government is all about and what its assurances of being willing to comply with the Minsk agreements are worth."

President Trump, for his part, in his Feb. 16 press conference, after repeated goading by the press to treat Russia as the enemy, respondaed:

> We're a very powerful nuclear country and so are they. I have been briefed. And I can tell you, one thing about a briefing that we're allowed to say, because anybody that ever read the most basic book can say it: nuclear holocaust would be like no other. They're a very powerful nuclear country, and so are we.

Dr. Natalia Vitrenko, the Ukrainian economist who has battled the Maidan regime from its outset, wrote in an open letter to Trump immediately after his election:

> I greatly hope that you will abandon, as undemocratic and intolerable, the planning and implementation of *coups d'état* through color revolutions, such as has been done by U.S. agencies twice in Ukraine. I would like to see you build relations with Russia and China not, as enemies or rivals, but as partners and allies in the name of peace, justice and prosperity for the entirety of

our planet Earth. I hope very much, that you will also make a positive influence on what is happening in Ukraine. Our people are suffering badly from war, extreme poverty, corruption, political repressions, and the rampaging of neo-Nazis. The outgoing U.S. Administration kept stirring up the people of Ukraine against Russia, thereby inciting a war between our fraternal peoples, one that unquestionably threatens to trigger a Third World War. The whole world awaits with hope, for you to carry out your promises with specific actions to ensure the welfare of every American and promote peace and prosperity for all mankind.

# Neo-Nazi Perpetrators of Regime Change

Feb. 20—The 2014 coup in Ukraine was perpetrated by figures and groups of the so-called opposition, whose lineage and practices trace directly to Nazi formations going back decades. Key parts of this network were fostered and protected by Britain's MI6, and the CIA, especially under Allen Dulles, as assets for geopolitical operations in Eastern Europe and against the Soviet, and later Russian states.

Among the most aggressive in the Euromaidan operation was the Right Sector, founded in November 2013 as a paramilitary confederation. It was made up of three groups, one of which, the Tryzub or Stepan Bandera Trident, was founded in 1993 by successors to the Hitler-aligned 1941 Organization of Ukrainian Nationalists-Bandera (OUN(b)), named for Stepan Bandera (1909-1959), the Ukrainian Hitlerite who founded his organization in Munich during WW II. The OUN itself goes back to the period of WW I, and its formal founding in 1929.

The 1941 proclamation by OUN(b) stated:

*The fascist Stepan Bandera, who fought with the Nazis against the Soviets. He was heroized by Euromaidan coup leaders.*

The newly formed Ukrainian state will work closely with the National-Socialist Greater Germany, under the leadership of its leader Adolf Hitler, which is forming a new order in Europe and the world, and is helping the Ukrainian people to free itself from Muscovite occupation....

In 1943, the military unit set up by Bandera's OUN(b) carried out a mass extermination campaign against Poles and Jews in Ukraine, killing an estimated 70,000 civilians during the Summer of that year alone. Nevertheless, by April 1948 Stepan Bandera was recruited to work for British intelligence, whose 1956 MI6 report described him as "a professional underground worker with a terrorist background and ruthless notions about rules of the game." Bandera's top official, Mykola Lebed, who carried out the Ukraine exterminations, went on to a CIA payroll as of 1948. Brought to New York City, Lebed headed a CIA front company, Prolog Research Corp., which was controlled during the 1950s by the CIA's Director of Plans, Frank Wisner. Various trainees and functions shifted to fronts in Europe over the coming years, including in Radio Liberty, and in London, the Society for Soviet Nationalist Studies (UK). It is this Bandera-Lebed legacy, and the networks spawned in the post-war period, which are at the center of the coup events in Ukraine and since.

The other two constituent groups of the Right Sector were the Ukrainian Patriot (UP), and the Ukrainian National Assembly-Ukrainian National Self-Defense (UNA-UNSO). The UP was founded in 1991 as the neo-Nazi youth wing of the Social-National Party of Ukraine, which in 2004 became the Svoboda (Freedom) Party, whose leaders were explicitly committed to

*Andriy Parubiy (l), Commandant of the Maidan, founded the Ukrainian Patriot youth group (1999), whose 2008 poster glorifies the Nazi 14th Waffen SS Division. Today he is Chairman of the Ukraine Parliament. Nadia Diuk (r) is VP of the National Endowment for Democracy.*

Wikimedia Commons

HolosAmeryky

government overthrow. UP members were famous for paramilitary training and confrontations, and deployed to the Maidan in December 2013.

Likewise, the UNA-UNSO and its youth arm, Bily Molot (White Hammer), both entered the Right Sector in November 2013. The group was founded in 1991 from various right-wing sub-groups, and its members ranged throughout eastern Europe in various violent confrontations.

The party and parliamentary leaders of these, and a few other organizations, played leading roles in the Euromaidan coup operation. Many went on to occupy key positions in the post-coup government, as their neo-Nazi organizations were absorbed into the military and bureaucracy. Those figures, with their affiliations, are noted below, and cited in the chronology immediately following. Also listed are two prominent U.S.-based backers of the coup, Natalia Diuk and Victoria Nuland.

**Dmytro Yarosh** became leader in 2007 of Tryzub (Stepan Bandera Trident) and then head of the Right Sector in November 2013. Earlier, on July 17, 2013, at the Tryzub training camp, he made a speech calling for a national revolution in Ukraine, and an end to the "Russian Empire." After the February 2014 coup, elements of the Right Sector came to be absorbed into various quasi-official battalions, like the Azov Battalion, in the National Guard of Ukraine.

**Andriy Parubiy** founded the Ukrainian Patriot (UP) youth group in 1999, which became a Right Sector unit in November 2013. He was Commandant of the Maidan. In the immediate post-coup government, he

became Secretary of the Ukrainian National Security and Defense Council. He is now Chairman of the Ukraine Parliament.

**Yuriy Lutsenko** was founder of the government-overthrow movement called TUR (Third Ukrainian Republic) which cited the earlier two republics as, first, that of 1917, and second, the 1941 Hitlerite Bandera-Stetsko Ukrainian State. (Yaroslav Stetsko was Bandera's deputy, and the declared head of the 1941 state; his widow Slava Stetsko, continued his work.) Today Lutsenko is Prosecutor General of Ukraine.

**Oleksandr Turchynov,** a parliamentarian for the Batkivshchyna (Fatherland) Party, was Speaker of the Rada, and was unconstitutionally installed as Acting President on Feb. 26, 2014, after the Feb. 18-22 coup, by a coalition government of the Svoboda and Fatherland parties. Today, Turchynov is Secretary of the National Security and Defense Council of Ukraine.

**Arseniy "Yats" Yatsenyuk,** a parliamentarian for the Batkivshchyna Party, was unconstitutionally installed on Feb. 26, 2014, as Prime Minister by the Batkivshchyna/Svoboda coalition. He held the position until April 2016.

**Vitali Klitschko** was a parliamentarian for the Udar Party (Ukrainian Democratic Alliance for Reforms), and a boxing champion. He is now Mayor of Kiev.

**Oleh Tyanybok** was a parliamentarian for the Svoboda Party.

**United States-based coup operatives:**

**Nadia Diuk,** as a young Ukrainian emigré in London in 1984, had very close contacts with Prolog Research, the CIA front group of Mykola Lebed, the security chief butcher for Stepan Bandera. She co-edited the Prolog-associated Soviet National Survey. In 1990, she joined the U.S. National Endowment for Democracy (NED), as Vice President for Africa, Central Europe, and Eurasia. Along the way, she married Adrian Karatnycky, also in the orbit of Prolog, who headed Freedom House for 12 years, and now is at the Atlantic Council. Diuk actively supported the Ukraine government overthrow process all along.

**Victoria Nuland** was Assistant Secretary of State for European and Eurasian Affairs (2013-2017), until dismissed by the Trump Administration in January. She was the lead Obama liaison for the 2014 color revolution coup in Ukraine. She served in previous posts, backing geopolitical intervention, in the name of "democracy." She was a foreign policy adviser to Vice President Dick Cheney (2003-2005), and Ambassador to NATO (2000-2003), during which time she strongly advocated NATO out-of-area deployments and similar operations. Her husband, Robert Kagan, is the neo-con co-founder of the Project for a New American Century (PNAC), which included targetting the nations of Iraq, Libya, Syria, and Yemen, to further the destabilization of Russia, India, and China.

# Chronology of the Coup

Feb. 20—A full chronology of the 2013-14 coup in Ukraine would have to begin at least with the 1947-52 quarrel between the U.S. Army Counterintelligence Corps (CIC), which tried to bar the "well-known sadist and collaborator of the Germans," Organization of Ukrainian Nationalists (OUN) figure Mykola Lebed, from entry into the United States, and CIA Deputy Director Allen Dulles, who ultimately secured permission for Lebed to come and go freely. In the view of Dulles, Lebed and the OUN were essential to Cold War operations against the Soviet Union.

Indeed, in recent months, historians and intelligence specialists have been perusing and publishing more and more freshly declassified documents on CIA and MI6 (British foreign intelligence) plans for anti-Soviet uprisings in Ukraine, in which they planned to utilize the OUN.

The continuation, in the post-Soviet period, of the OUN, its ideology, and its plans for the takeover of Ukraine and an ultimate showdown with Russia, are summarized elsewhere in this report. The timeline below is but one slice, covering the active coup period of Nov. 21, 2013 through Feb. 22, 2014. The core of it appeared in **EIR** of May 16, 2014, where it served to disprove assertions such as that of then-Assistant Secretary of State Victoria Nuland, who on Jan. 15, 2014, portrayed the brewing "Euromaidan" coup in Kiev as a spontaneous democratic upsurge:

> [T]he movement that started as a demand for a European future grew into a protest for basic human dignity and justice, clean and account-

able government, and economic and political independence of Ukraine.

The allegation that a violent coup was pre-planned is confirmed by very diverse sources.

Former intelligence officer, now Russian President Vladimir Putin, spoke Dec. 2, 2013 about the events beginning to unfold:

> [E]verything that is happening now is not a revolution, but a well-organized protest. And in my view, these events were not prepared for today, but for the Presidential election campaign of Spring 2015. What's happening now is just a little false start due to certain circumstances, but is also preparations for the Presidential election. The fact that these are preparations is obvious to all objective observers, judging from what we see on television, how well-organized and trained militant groups actually operate. That's my assessment.

From the inside, no one was more explicit than Right Sector leader Dmytro Yarosh. On July 17, 2013, during the annual summer paramilitary training camp for his cadre, Yarosh video-recorded a speech that circulated widely online. It contained three summary points:

1. There is an "internal occupation" regime in Ukraine;

2. No liberation of the Ukrainian people and no Ukrainian statehood is possible without a national revolution; and

3. Russia is the age-old enemy of Ukraine and "as long as the Russian Empire exists in any form, true, real national independence of Ukraine and the Ukrainian people is impossible."

Then Yarosh made a forecast:

The times are coming, when we will not only be talking and conducting various propaganda actions about the national revolution, but the times are coming that will forge history and fix the footprint of our people in the existence of the Ukrainian nation. We must show not only in words, but with our deeds, that the Bandera cause is not yesterday, but it is the present and the future.... The times are approaching that we may have been only dreaming about for these 20 years. Because we can win, we want to win, and we shall win.

Wikimedia Commons

*A supporter of Hitler-collaborator Stepan Bandera (on the poster) marches on the Maidan, 2013.*

The sources for the following items include contemporary Ukrainian media reports on the *Zerkalo Nedeli* site (zn.ua), Facebook pages of the quoted persons, YouTube postings, and Euromaidan live streams from Espreso TV and Hromadske TV.

## November 2013

On Nov. 21, a few hundred people gathered in Independence Square known as Maidan in Kiev, on the occasion of the halt in the process of Ukraine signing a formal Association Agreement with the EU. Early on, large numbers of people turned out, waving EU flags, looking to the EU for a way out of the hardship from the shock therapy of the 1990s, and the privatization/IMF austerity continued through the 2004 Orange Revolution years. But beyond the initial size of the turnout, the pre-planned Right Sector and other Banderite paramilitary violence was then used for systematic escalation of the Maidan. Among the prominent figures on Nov. 21 was Andriy Parubiy, an active Banderite radical for more than two decades, and Yuri Lutsenko, an organizer of the 2004 Orange Revolution Maidan, after which he held office as Minister of Internal Affairs, was jailed in 2011 for abuse of office, and released in 2013.

On Nov. 24, Lutsenko called on people to stay in the Square through Nov. 29, the day the EU Association Agreement was to have been signed by President Yanukovych.

On Nov. 29, the first escalation took place. When, at night, the protest had wound down to only a few hundred people remaining in the Maidan, suddenly a thousand Berkut police ("Golden Eagle," an elite riot force) showed up, and just as suddenly, unidentified persons rushed the police, attacking them with chains. The brutal Berkut retaliation, with beatings of young people, was filmed and broadcast widely on television and social media. In subsequent analysis, observers from all sides have pointed to the role of Yanukovych's then-Chief of Staff Serhiy Lyovochkin in staging this provocation. Some suggest he wanted to spark violence in order to generate a pretext for ending the Maidan by force, while others point to Lyovochkin's Washington ties and believe he was acting for those abroad who wanted to escalate the crisis.

On Nov. 30, Lutsenko called for blockading central Kiev until Yanukovych stepped down. The same day, British envoy Catherine Ashton, EU High Representative for Foreign Affairs and Security Policy, issued a joint statement with EU official Stefan Füle condemning "the excessive use of force last night by the police in Kiev to disperse peaceful protesters," who were calling for integrating Ukraine with the EU.

## December 2013

On Dec. 1, Lutsenko told the rally, "Our plan is clear: This is no longer a rally or a protest action. This is a revolution."

On Dec. 2, Lutsenko announced that Maidan Self-

Defense Forces were operational. "We have units who will be able to defend the people," he said. "As many as we need…well-prepared, specially trained people, who are taking responsibility for physical defense against possible attack."

On Dec. 8, Parubiy declared, "Neither the government, nor Yanukovych, nor anybody else will be able to work, until our demands are met. We are standing here till victory."

On Dec. 10, U.S. Assistant Secretary of State Victoria Nuland and Catherine Ashton of the EU were in Kiev. Nuland went to the Maidan, distributing food to the protestors. This was one of three trips to Kiev that Nuland made over November and December, supporting the protesters.

On Dec. 11, Secretary of State John Kerry denounced the actions of riot police.

On Dec. 12, Parubiy was now referred to in the media as Commandant of the Maidan. He announced plans to expand the tent city there and to reinforce the barricades.

On Dec. 13, Victoria Nuland addressed a Washington, D.C. National Press Club event, stating:

Since the declaration of Ukrainian independence in 1991, the United States supported the Ukrainians in the development of democratic institutions and skills in promoting civil society and a good form of government….

We have invested more than $5 billion dollars to help Ukraine achieve these and other goals….

On Dec. 22, the creation of "Maidan" as a formal organization was announced by Rada parliamentarian Tyahnybok, of Svoboda. He said, "Next we'll do guerrilla operations to blockade government buildings and make it impossible for the scoundrels now in power to live or sleep." Lutsenko called for spreading the "territory of the Maidan" to central Ukraine by Spring, reaching Crimea during the Summer. Officers of the Maidan were named.

## January 2014

On Jan. 1, the second violent escalation took place. Three days after measures were put through the Parlia-

*Blazing barricades in Kiev, Jan. 19, 2014. Western press coverage almost universally attributed the violence to "police brutality."*

Wikimedia Commons/Mystslav Chernov

ment outlawing many Maidan violent practices, Right Sector squads attacked the Berkut forces around the government quarter itself. This action on Hrushevsky Street then began several days of violence, bringing the first deaths.

On Jan. 4, Parubiy, warning of coming attempts to break up the Maidan, said that "right after the holidays will be a good period for our switchover to the offensive."

On Jan. 15, Victoria Nuland praised the Maidan uprising.

The movement that started as a demand for a European future, grew into a protest for basic human dignity and justice, clean and accountable government, and economic and political independence for Ukraine.

From Jan. 22 onward, shocking images came forth of policemen set on fire by napalm-like Molotov cocktails. Kiev was swathed in black smoke from burning piles of tires, ignited by the Maidan fighters. The U.S. National Security Council (NSC), however, downplayed the violence as expressing "the legitimate grievances of the people." NSC spokesperson Caitlyn Hayden threatened the Ukraine government with sanctions, if the riot police were not withdrawn from the Maidan.

On Jan. 25, Parubiy told *Deutsche Welle* that the revolution was approaching "its victorious conclusion." He described how the Maidan Self-Defense

Forces were organized in a *sotnya* structure (hundred-man units) and combat-ready.

On Jan. 28, amid demands by the government that the demonstrators relinquish the government buildings they had occupied, Parubiy declared that President Yanukovych had better release his Presidential office on Bankovaya Street. "They release Bankovaya, and we'll release the October Palace," Parubiy said. "I think those are good starting points for negotiations."

On Jan. 29, the formation of a National Guard was announced at the Maidan. It comprised the Maidan Self-Defense Forces, Right Sector, and unspecified Cossacks.

## February 2014

On Feb. 3, Nadia Diuk had a signed article in the *Kyiv Post*, "Ukraine's Self-Organizing Revolution," praising the Euromaidan process. She spoke as Vice President of the U.S. government-backed National Endowment for Democracy.

On Feb. 4, a phone taping was posted on YouTube, between Victoria Nuland and U.S. Ambassador to Ukraine Geoffrey Pyatt, in which Nuland spoke of whom she wanted as Ukraine head of government. Referring to Parliament members Vitali Klitschko as "Klitsch" and Arseniy Yatsenuk as "Yats," she stated, "I don't think Klitsch should go into the government. I don't think it's necessary. I don't think it's a good idea. I think Yats is the guy ."

Then, referring to Ban Ki-moon's interventions compared to those of the EU regarding Ukraine, Nuland said, "and, you know, fuck the EU."

On Feb. 7, Parubiy stated that the Maidan Self-Defense force, now numbering 12,000, would become a nationwide organization. Because under current law their organization was illegal, they would not seek legalization, but would change the regime.

On Feb. 11, Parubiy signed Order #1, "On the Fundamental Organizational Principles of the Maidan Self-Defense," posted on Facebook. Its objectives included, "to resist the current criminal regime until its complete elimination."

On Feb. 18 came the third escalation, in which by the end of the day 25 people were dead. The events began when the Maidan leaders and Tyahnybok of Svoboda announced a "peaceful march" to the Parliament to make sure it adopted the "correct" decisions, namely, to curtail presidential powers (by returning to the Constitution of 2004). As the procession approached the police lines around the Rada, again along Hrushevsky Street, the "peaceful" marchers went on the attack. This began hours of street fighting, in which 25 people were killed.

Late on the night of Feb. 19, a truce was announced after negotiations between the Parliamentary opposition trio of Yatsenyuk, Klitschko, and Tyahnybok, and President Yanukovych.

Overnight, Parubiy and Yarosh rejected it. Yarosh wrote on Facebook, "In the event that the internal occupation forces of the Ministry of Internal Affairs cease fire and the Supreme Rada of Ukraine immediately cancels the dictatorial powers of Yanukovych, we shall apply maximum efforts to bring the bloodshed to a halt and guarantee their safety."

On Feb. 20, in the early morning, shots were fired from the Conservatory building where Parubiy and Maidan commanders had relocated after their former location in the Trade Union building had burned. The shots hit police and demonstrators. An all-day gun battle began, in which another 70 people died amid unidentified sniper fire.

On Feb. 21, the opposition MP trio and President Yanukovych signed an agreement, witnessed by the foreign ministers of Germany, France, and Poland, committing to constitutional reform by September, Presidential elections late in the year, and turning in of weapons.

When the document was then taken to the Maidan, it was booed. After a fire-brand speech against the agreement by the young commander of a Maidan Self-Defense *sotnya* from Lviv, Volodymyr Parasyuk, the deal was off. Instead, if Yanukovych did not resign by 10 a.m. the next morning, Parasyuk shouted, his *sotnya* was ready to go on full attack against the government.

Yanukovych left Kiev during the night, travelling first to Kharkov, then to his native Donetsk, and then, with Russian assistance, taking refuge in Crimea for several days, and eventually in Russia.

On Feb. 22, the Rada unconstitutionally installed Oleksandr Turchynov, of the All-Ukrainian Union (Fatherland) Party, as acting prime minister, then as acting President the next day.

On Feb. 23, in the evening, Yuri Lutsenko took the microphone on the Maidan stage and thanked a long list of those who had made possible the ouster of the elected President of Ukraine (without the impeachment procedure defined in the Constitution). Lutsenko offered special gratitude to "Right Sector and its leader, Dmytro Yarosh."

# Color Revolutions—Acts of War

Feb. 20—The fomenting of "color revolutions" to bring down governments or nations is an act of war. The strategy was developed, and is being actively promoted out of institutions centered in the neo-British Empire, particularly at Oxford, home of the Civil Resistance and Power Politics project, and in associated networks based in the United States, such as the National Endowment for Democracy (NED). The money flows come from direct government sources e.g., NED is funded by Congress, and private agencies and donors, such as billionaire George Soros.

In its latest application, a color revolution operation is currently being conducted as an attempted coup against the government of the United States, manifest in the various forms of mob-think, and mob-defiance against the President, to prevent the United States from breaking into a new system of foreign relations for peace and economic development, and in particular to cooperate with Russia and China on defeating terrorism, and building infrastructure as part of the New Silk Road.

A major funder of these coup operations is Wall Street megaspeculator George Soros, who has openly stated his desire to see President Trump out of office.

The color revolution method is simple, and ancient. Instigate and manipulate a frenzied mob around simplistic demands to accomplish whatever geopolitical goals are intended:

- Ousting of a president,
- Overthrow of governments,
- Creation of chaos,
- Provocations to war.

The term "color" refers to how a single color, symbol, slogan, or demand is promoted and repeated, to inflame passion and retard reason.

The map of successful examples includes the "Rose Revolution" in Georgia (2003), the Orange Revolution in Ukraine (2004), and the like, going back to such earlier examples as the 1986 overthrow of Ferdinand Marcos in the Philippines, whose banner was "yellow." These and other cases reveal the activities open and covert by think-tanks and irregular warfare operatives, to accomplish evil objectives.

Look more closely at the British nexus. In 2006, two Oxford professors, Sir Adam Roberts and Timothy Garton Ash, created a project called Civil Resistance

EIRNS/Stuart Lewis

*The biggest private financier of "democracy" movements is the London-Wall Street moneybags George Soros. His foundations pump hundreds of millions of dollars annually into "civil society" operations in target nations, and inside the United States, as well as pushing dope legalization.*

and Power Politics: Domestic and International Dimensions (CRPP).

They churn out books, conferences, and trainees in the methods of government subversion, done under various names, such as "democracy promotion," or furthering the "liberal international order." The predecessors of these modern Oxford operations go back to British Empire colonial times, when not only direct military subjugation was used, but also indirect rule by manipulating the public outlook.

In the United States, the National Endowment for Democracy (NED), founded in 1983, is in the lead of operations to sponsor "civil society" groups in dozens of countries, for purposes hiding behind the name of promoting democracy or furthering whatever kind of "people power" subversion they choose. Nations which are subservient to the British imperial order, such as Saudi Arabia, are not touched regardless of their disdain for "democracy."

The NED today boasts of making more than 1,200 grants yearly, to support "the projects of non-governmental groups abroad who are working for 'democratic' goals in more than 90 countries." The NED and other agencies function under the "Project Democracy" banner, which was formally initiated in 1983 by the U.S. Information Agency, to give fellowships and conduct activities abroad.

Among the interconnections between the Oxford crowd and U.S. operations, are many personnel. For example, Nadia Diuk, NED Vice President for Programs for Africa, Europe, and Eurasia, whose biography boasts of how she has specialized in "strategies for the underground democratic movements before 1989" in Yugoslavia, and beyond. Diuk studied at Oxford with the "democratizers," and mixed it up in London with the U.S. and British-backed Ukrainian fascist networks. Her role is typical of British-associated functionaries in U.S. institutions.

## Victoria Nuland

Victoria Nuland at the State Department, was point person for the U.S. support of the Ukrainian Maidan operation. On Dec. 13, 2014, in the midst of the violent anti-government confrontation in Kiev, Nuland spoke in Washington, D.C., saying:

> Since Ukraine's independence in 1991, the United States has supported Ukrainians as they build democratic skills and institutions, as they promote civic participation and good governance, all of which are preconditions for Ukraine to achieve its European aspirations. We have invested over $5 billion to assist Ukraine in these and other goals....

The biggest private financier of "democracy" movement subversion, is the London-Wall Street billionaire George Soros. His overall agency is the Open Society Foundations, based in New York City, which has pumped hundreds of millions into target locations, such as eastern Europe, for purposes seen in the 2014 overthrow of the elected government of Ukraine.

Soros has openly declared Russian President Vladimir Putin to be more dangerous than ISIS, and is the primary funder of the mass, mindless demonstrations in the United States today, working with Obama, aimed at bringing down the Trump government and returning to "regime change wars" and nuclear confrontation with Russia. (See Soros's article, "Putin Is a Bigger Threat to Europe Than Isis," in *The Guardian, Feb. 11.*)

Soros's own connection with European Nazi networks is personal, going back to his youth in Hungary, when he and his father chose to hide their Jewish heri-

*Gene Sharp, operating from his Albert Einstein Institution in Boston, is known as the author of the color revolution strategy for deployment against target governments.*

tage and work with the Nazi occupation to confiscate the property of fellow Jews who had been sent to the concentration camps, an experience he has described as a useful life experience. Another long-standing focus of his Open Society interventions is the promotion of the legalization of psychotropic drugs.

In the United States, the longtime guru for "people power" and government overthrow is Gene Sharp, based in Boston. In 1968, he did his Oxford doctoral dissertation, *From Dictatorship to Democracy: A Conceptual Framework for Liberation.* Then in 1973, he produced a three-volume color-revolution playbook, titled *The Politics of Non-Violent Action.* His writings, translated into more than 40 languages, provide a boiled-down list of 198 items, which he calls political defiance tactics (PD).

The Sharp tactics range from boycotts to symbolism, including: "Display of symbolic Colors," "Protest disrobings," "Symbolic lights," "Paint as protest," "Rude gestures," and so forth.

These color revolution tactics are now in full play in the United States, in the anti-Trump "resistance" movement. Instead of bringing forward policies and furthering debate, agitation networks are pushing street actions, slogans ("Stand Up," "Not My President," "Shame"), and violence.

On Jan. 30, the recently announced group "Indivisible" released a 25-page "Practical Guide" on how to conduct mass protest, i.e., applied political defiance. While the Indivisibles deny receiving Soros money directly, some of its founders have been directly on the

Soros payroll. For example, top leader Angel Padilla, an analyst with the National Immigration Law Center, is financed by the Open Society Foundations. Indivisible has links with the Soros-funded MoveOn.org and the Working Families Party, all three of which held their first nationwide conference call for activists on Jan. 22. The theme is to "resist," not to have a policy mission.

Obama himself, incredibly, is bombarding Americans with robocalls attacking President Trump, and encouraging protests and demonstrations against the President; Obama's "Organizing for Action" national network is organizing those demonstrations and disruptions of Congressional town hall meetings. This is Obama's personal support and funds network, working to bring down the President of the United States, to return to Obama's perpetual war policy and military confrontation with Russia.

### Cui Bono?

Who benefits? Those who are desperate to prevent the United States from linking up with the drive for world development underway in the global "New Silk Road" led by Chinese President Xi Jinping and Russian President Vladimir Putin, and to end the military confrontation with Russia in favor of cooperation in development and in defeating terrorism. President Trump has shown inclinations to link up, which is anathema to the dying British system of monetarism and geopolitics. So the full color revolution apparatus is now deployed against the United States, from within.

It is time to understand the truth of the color revolution warfare deployed against Ukraine, and Russia, three years ago, and how the same networks are now committing warfare against Americans at home. We can stop this, and make way for a future for all nations.

# New Frame-up Attempt Against Vitrenko in Ukraine

Feb. 10—Ukrainian economist and former MP, Dr. Natalia Vitrenko, appealed today to the High Representative of the European Union for Foreign Affairs and Security Policy, Federica Mogherini, to take action against the "defamation, intimidation, persecution, and discrediting", to which Vitrenko and her political party are being subjected in violation of the European Convention on Human Rights.

In a video posted Feb. 8, titled "Ukrainian Terror instead of European Democracy," Vitrenko presented the latest evidence that the Ukraine Security Service (SBU) is attempting to silence her through a politically motivated frame-up on criminal charges of separatism. Ukrainian law defines as a crime "infringement of the territorial integrity of Ukraine." The law was instituted after the U.S.-backed coup that overthrew Ukraine's elected President Victor Yanukovych, the third anniversary of which comes on Feb. 22.

On Oct. 28, 2016, the offices of Vitrenko's Progressive Socialist Party of Ukraine (PSPU) were raided and occupied by paramilitary forces, acting in a real estate dispute involving the building's landlord. The contents of the office property of the PSPU, its newspaper, as-sociated organizations, and individual members were carted off and sequestered by the SBU. In November, Vitrenko had warned that the SBU could be combing through the confiscated computer files for evidence to use in reviving a 2014 criminal investigation of the Gift of Life women's NGO, and Vitrenko personally as its head, on false charges of "infringing the territorial integrity of Ukraine." This is Article 110 of the Criminal Code of Ukraine, which carries a penalty of 10 years in prison.

Dr. Vitrenko was interrogated by the SBU twice in 2014, regarding their charges that the Gift of Life organization had received Russian funds for the purpose of engaging in what some media maliciously depicted as "propaganda work to discredit the Ukrainian government authorities, provoke armed conflict between different layers of the population of Ukraine, incite ethnic hatred, and provide informational support for conducting 'referenda' in Ukraine's eastern regions." In April 2015, after Vitrenko had strongly refuted the charges during her interrogation, and the investigation had languished for a year, the Glavcom news agency (glavcom.ua) fanned its flames again, with several articles citing SBU "suspicions" about Vitrenko's receiving money from the Russian Foreign Ministry-run Fund for the Support and Defense of the Rights of Compatriots Residing Abroad. The allegations date to May 2014, when the bank accounts of Gift of Life were frozen. According to Ukrainian media, this was done "in the framework of an SBU investigation of funds transfers through Ukrinbank, intended for persons suspected of infringement of the territorial integrity and inviolability of Ukraine." A flood of media reports named Vitrenko as a major sponsor of separatists and terrorists, which are broad categories used by the current Ukrainian authorities against their political opponents.

www.vitrenko.org

*Natalia Vitrenko at a rally of her party, the Progressive Socialist Party of Ukraine.*

The PSPU said in a statement on April 8, 2015:

It is no accident, that this falsehood has been disseminated. The regime brought to power by the Euromaidan is discrediting itself through economic collapse, social genocide, corruption, and its inability to establish peace and preserve the territorial integrity of the country or realize the promised European values. Natalia Vitrenko offered facts to prove that the 'suspicions' are invalid and the statements false. But efforts to defame her and shape a negative view of her on the part of the public are continuing, through the media.

Once again at the end of 2016, it appears that the SBU did not find what it wanted in the material seized during the raid on PSPU headquarters. Instead, on Feb. 4, Vitrenko learned through an article in Glavcom with the incendiary headline "Court seizes property of organization headed by Vitrenko: infringement of the territorial integrity of Ukraine suspected," that the SBU is plunging ahead with its case, based on entirely fake evidence. The article claimed that on Jan. 23, a Kiev court, having reviewed a motion filed by an SBU investigator, had ordered the seizure of property belonging to Gift of Life. The court order, however, listed property confiscated at a different location in Kiev, and to which

the Gift of Life organization had no connection whatsoever: tents, sleeping bags, bottles ("Are they trying to make it sound like a Molotov cocktail factory?" Vitrenko asks in her new video), and boxes of dried pasta.

Pointing out that the Ukrainian Constitution guarantees citizens protection against false accusations, Vitrenko, in the video, details what the human rights defense activity of Gift of Life (founded in 2000) actually was in 2012-14, at which point it had to cease operations because the SBU caused its accounts to be frozen. She wages a polemic in the video, that if her economic program had been adopted by Ukraine in the mid-1990s, when as a member of Parliament, she issued it in opposition to International Monetary Fund-prescribed deregulation and privatization, Ukraine would have been a thriving nation today; there would have been no economic hardship, such as made people fall for the "better life in Europe" slogans of the coup organizers, and thus there would have been no coup, no loss of Crimea, and no uprising in the Donbass leading to the deaths of 10,000 people.

Far from "infringing" anything, Vitrenko states that her program would have protected Ukraine and guaranteed its future prosperity in cooperation with Eurasian development overall.

Vitrenko has demanded a retraction of the Feb. 4 article on the Glavcom website. The text of her appeal to Mogherini follows.

# PSPU Appeal: Stop the Defamation of a Ukrainian Opposition Party!

*The letter below was sent on Feb. 10, 2017, to the High Representative of the European Union for Foreign Affairs and Security Policy Federica Mogherini. Its full title is, "Appeal of the PSPU Central Committee: Help stop the defamation of a Ukrainian opposition party and its leader Natalia Vitrenko!" Copies were directed to the Kiev Embassies of Belarus, China, France, Germany, Italy, Russia, and the U.S.A., as well as to Ukraine's President Petro Poroshenko, the heads of his Ministry of Internal Affairs, Security Service, and Prosecutor General's Office, and the Ukrainian Parliament's Human Rights Ombudsman.*

The CC PSPU appeals to you to act for the cessation of the political defamation of an opposition party, the Progressive Socialist Party of Ukraine, and its leader, Doctor of Economics, Peoples Deputy of Ukraine in the 2nd and 3rd Convocations, and first female Presidential candidate in the history of Ukraine, Natalia Vitrenko. Despite the fact that Ukraine has signed and ratified an Association Agreement with the European Union and has assumed the obligation to ensure implementation of the norms and principles of European democracy (freedom of peaceful assembly, freedom of political activity, political pluralism, the right to a fair trial, the supremacy of law, the right to respect for one's private life, the right to peacefully possess property, and the presumption of innocence), a policy of defamation, intimidation, persecution, and discreditation is being carried out against our Progressive Socialist Party of Ukraine, an opposition party. Its result is to hinder the political activity of our party. We offer several examples by way of demonstration:

1. The Ministry of Justice of Ukraine has twice refused to register the decisions of the XXIX (8 Sept. 2015) and XXX (25 June 2016) Congresses of the PSPU on amending the Program and Charter of the PSPU in accordance with the requirements of the Law of Ukraine "On the condemnation of communist and national-socialist (Nazi) totalitarian regimes in Ukraine and the prohibition of propaganda of their symbols." The Ministry confronts the PSPU with unfounded claims, demonstratively refusing to work constructively on preparing the Congress documents.

2. The Ministry of Justice of Ukraine, ignoring the PSPU's appeal, refuses to enter amendments to the composition of the party's governing bodies as listed in the Register of Public Associations, which directly affects the legitimacy of the activity of the Central Committee of the PSPU, essentially blocking the activity of the party under its Charter.

3. Law enforcement agencies of Ukraine have conducted no investigation and have charged nobody in:

• The beating, by Nazis from the Azov Battalion, of participants in a peaceful demonstration organized by the PSPU on 17 March 2016 in Kyiv;

• The forcible interference by neo-Nazis in the conduct of a legal peaceful demonstration by the PSPU on 9 May 2016 in Kyiv and the destruction of the PSPU's party symbols.

4. The Security Service, Prosecutor's Office, Ministry of Internal Affairs and courts of Ukraine, by their decisions, actions, and illegal non-action, allowed citizen A.E. Shatilin and neo-Nazis from the Azov Battalion to seize the premises of the PSPU's central office on 28 October 2016, which had been rented since 2005 from the legal owner of the premises, the Siver Ukraina company. Tenants, besides the PSPU, also included other legal entities: the editorial offices of the PSPU newspaper Dosvitni Ogni, the all-Ukraine women's public organization Dar zhizni (Gift of Life), the all-Ukraine public organization (AUPO) Eurasian People's Union, and the public organization (PO) Assembly of Orthodox Women of Ukraine. In addition to seizure of the premises, also seized were the PSPU's charter documents, letterhead, party cards, and the seal of the PSPU, party literature, party symbols, the party's archive of its 20 years of activity, computer and duplicating equipment, personal data of the governing bodies and membership of the party, and personal belongings of PSPU Chairman N. Vitrenko and PSPU Deputy Chairman V. Marchenko.

The day after seizure of the premises, on 29 October 2016 an SBU investigator, in coordination with the prosecutor's office, without a warrant, without a court ruling in its favor, and without informing the PSPU or the all-Ukraine women's organization (AUWO) Dar Zhizni, conducted a research, resulting in the confiscation of property of the party and the Editorial Board of the PSPU party newspaper: hard disks with political journalistic information of the newspaper's Editorial Board, literature, party documents, and personal belongings of Natalia Vitrenko and Vladimir Marchenko. The search and seizure of this property was conducted in the absence of any criminal or administrative claims against the PSPU, but under the framework of a falsely fabricated criminal case, opened back in April 2014 against the AUWO Dar Zhizni, headed by Natalia Vitrenko. This politically motivated, completely unfounded and unproven criminal case had in effect been frozen for two and a half years.

A criminal case was opened on 29 October 2016 in the matter of the seizure of the premises and property of the PSPU and the editorial offices of the party newspaper; on 12 December 2016 the PSPU and the Editorial Board of Dosvitni ogni, the AUWO Dar Zhizni, the AUPO Eurasian People's Union, and the PO Assembly of Orthodox Women of Ukraine, as well as N. Vitrenko and V. Marchenko personally, were recognized as aggrieved parties.

Nonetheless, neither the investigator in that case, the prosecutor's office, nor the SBU has taken any action since that time (three and a half months!) in defense of the interests of the PSPU, the Editorial Board of the party newspaper, the public organizations, and the party leadership.

The appeals of PSPU Chairman N. Vitrenko to President of Ukraine P. Poroshenko, Prosecutor General of Ukraine Yu. Lutsenko, head of the Security Service of Ukraine V. Hrytsak did not prompt them to defend the rights of the political party, the public organizations, or the journalists.

In effect the PSPU has been deprived of the possibility of defending its rights in court. Even the legal owner of the premises, the Siver Ukraina company, is unable to lodge a complaint against the search and property-seizure actions of the SBU and the prosecutor's office, because the case has not been transferred from the primary court (the Pechersky District Court of the city of Kyiv) to the Appeals Court of the city of Kyiv for two months, so far.

5. Furthermore, the Security Service of Ukraine and the prosecutor's office, with the assistance of the investigating judge of the Pechersky District of the city of Kyiv, carried out searches on 18 November 2016 and 20 January 2016, and on 23 January 2017 property was seized by order of the court property of persons unknown and having nothing whatsoever to do with the PSPU, Natalia Vitrenko, or the women's organization she heads. This search and seizure was done, it bears repeating, under the falsely fabricated criminal case against the all-Ukraine women's public organization Dar Zhizni, which the Ukrainian government continues to use for purposes of defaming N. Vitrenko, accusing her of infringing the territorial integrity of Ukraine.

6. The Ukrainian media, carrying out political instructions to defame N. Vitrenko and make her a target for terrorists, publish false information on the basis of information from the SBU and the prosecutor's office, and ascribe non-existent crimes to Natalia Vitrenko.

The Central Committee of the Progressive Socialist Party of Ukraine is convinced that these actions by the Ukrainian authorities are politically motivated, for the purpose of impeding the activity of this opposition political party and its leader, Doctor of Economics, People's Deputy of Ukraine in the 2nd and 3rd convocations, and first female Presidential candidate in the history of Ukraine Natalia Mikhailovna Vitrenko. The CC PSPU asks you to consider our Appeal to help the PSPU, the Editorial Board of Dosvitni Ogni newspaper, and the other public organizations named above, to carry out their lawful activity in accordance with the European Convention on Human Rights and the practice of the European Court of Human Rights, which the nation of Ukraine has undertaken the obligation to honor.

On behalf of the CC PSPU,
Chairman of the PSPU, Natalia Vitrenko

—*Compiled by EIR staff: Michael Billington, Rachel Douglas, and Marcia Merry Baker*

**For Further Reference**

Western Powers Back Neo-Nazi Coup in Ukraine (*EIR*, Feb. 7, 2014)

British Imperial Project in Ukraine: Violent Coup, Fascist Axioms (*EIR*, May 16, 2014)

Moscow Conference Identifies 'Color Revolutions' as War, by Tony Papert (2014)

Ukraine: A Post-Modernist Revolution, by Konstantin Cheremnykh (2005)

Ukrainian Economist Natalia Vitrenko: Finding a Noble Path out of the Crisis (*EIR*, Nov. 6, 2009)

Ukrainian Patriots Expose EU Support for Neo-Nazi Coup (*EIR*, March 7, 2014), a transcript of Vitrenko webcast, made in Paris on Feb. 24, 2014, i.e., two days after the coup).

# Every Day Counts In Today's Showdown To Save Civilization

# II. The New Paradigm

# China-Pakistan Economic Corridor: Major Asian Connectivity in Progress

by Ramtanu Maitra

Feb. 19—The China-Pakistan Economic Corridor (CPEC) is a proposed road-based transport system that will link China's western province of Xinjiang to Pakistan and will then extend southwestward through Pakistan to reach the Arabian Sea. That is its basic form. It will not be a single highway, but a network. It begins as a single road at the border with China, and then branches out into a number of routes traversing the length of Pakistan while covering the country from west to east (see map). But it is also more than a network of roads—it includes two dozen projects for the construction of power plants and power transmission lines.

Of equal importance is CPEC's objective to reach the Arabian Sea, near the Gulf of Oman, thereby connecting the land route to the other arm of China's One Belt, One Road project for connectivity and trade, the Maritime Silk Road.

To achieve that end, China has put special emphasis on developing a sleepy fishing village, Gwadar, located on the Makran coast of Balochistan province, into a major Pakistani port. This village and its surrounding region, which Pakistan bought in 1950 from the Sultanate of Oman, remained a traditional fishing village until China took over its development in 2007, years before the agreement for the CPEC was signed. After its first-stage development, Pakistan leased Gwadar to China until 2059, and China has reportedly invested about

CC/Kumail Ali Naqvi

*The border crossing in the Khunjerab (or Khunjrab) Pass on the northern border of Pakistan. You are now entering China.*

$1.6 billion so far to make it operational as a deepwater port.

The CPEC project took off in July 2013, when China and Pakistan signed a landmark agreement enabling China to construct an economic corridor linking Kashgar in Xinjiang to Gwadar on the Arabian Sea. In the north, the economic corridor will enter Pakistan from China through Gilgit-Baltistan—the part of the disputed state of Jammu and Kashmir that is under Pakistani administration—and will wind its multiple ways through all four Pakistani provinces to reach the Arabian Sea in the south. CPEC, in its proposed form, is expected to be wholly functional around 2028. Of the many constituent projects that make up the CPEC, a few are already finished and numerous others are now under construction. In November 2016, the CPEC's potential was signaled when Chinese cargo travelled by road to Gwadar Port for maritime transshipment to Africa and West Asia.

The estimated cost to develop this highway system—and the associated infrastructure and energy projects necessary to make the CPEC a success—was put at $46 billion in 2014, although cost overruns are generally expected. China's state-owned banks are financing Chinese companies to build, maintain, and operate the highways and associated infrastructure and energy projects in Pakistan over the next few years. Of that amount, $33.8 billion will be invested in energy projects and $11.8 billion in building the highways and associated infrastructure, such as upgrading railroads and even setting up a desalination plant. But the $46 billion investment figure is not an amount etched on granite.

Since 2014, China has come up with projects worth another $ 8.5 billion. Pakistan's Planning Minister, Ahsan Iqbal, in an interview with Reuters in November 2016, said "some $4.5 billion of the additional investment will be spent on upgrading tracks and signaling on the railway line from Karachi to Peshawar [about 1340 km or 833 miles] and increase the speed on the line to 160 km per hour [100 mph] from the current 60-80 kph." Another $4 billion will go toward a liquefied natural gas (LNG) terminal and transmission line, he added. "This has now all been approved, so this is an additional $8.5 billion to the $46 billion we had already, so we are now close to $55 billion," Ahsan said.

## A Win-Win Project

In 2013, when China's President Xi Jinping proposed the CPEC, it became evident that this economic corridor would be significantly different from the China-Central Asia corridor or the China-Russia-Europe corridor, both based on railroads. Broadly speaking, the CPEC project has two major elements. First, Gwadar Port is important in China's future plans. Gwadar will enable China to bring oil and gas overland from the Persian Gulf to develop its western regions and avoid further crowding of the already crowded Malacca Strait that connects the Indian Ocean to the South China Sea. Gwadar is just 400 km from the Strait of Hormuz, a major

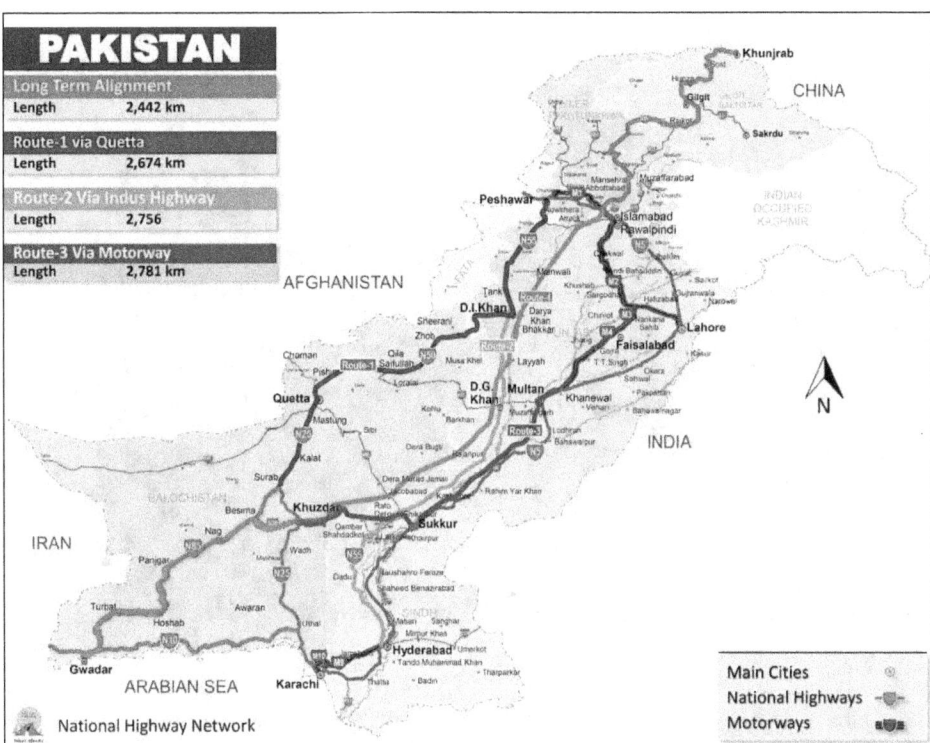

The China-Pakistan Economic Corridor comprises multiple routes from the border with China to the deep-water port at Gwadar.

world oil supply line, and is 1,500 km from Kashgar, China. Pipeline construction from Gwadar to Kashgar is to begin this year.

When the CPEC becomes fully operational, a significant part of China's oil imports from the Persian Gulf—which amount to about 60 percent of China's overall oil imports today—will come in through this route. The distance from the Strait of Hormuz to Kashgar via the CPEC is 2,000 km, as opposed to the 12,000 km of maritime distance from the Strait of Hormuz to

Gwadar opened as an international port, Nov. 13, 2016.

A textile mill in Punjab.

The Nation, Lahore, Pakistan

the eastern Chinese port of Shanghai via the Strait of Malacca. Oil or LNG landed at *any* port in China, if its destination is China's west, must then be carried westward overland for additional thousands of kilometers. The CPEC cuts both distance and time. Gwadar Port will also enable China to carry out two-way trade more efficiently with the nations along Africa's eastern coast, as well with the Persian Gulf countries west of Pakistan.

The second element of the CPEC is that it will improve Pakistan's stability by helping it to strengthen, and in some cases build, its physical and industrial infrastructure. Pakistan, in many ways, is at a different developmental level than the Central Asian states, although it is not as rich in natural resources as the "stan" countries. Some factors behind this difference are these:

• Pakistan has a population close to 185 million (the Central Asian nations and Afghanistan together have less than 100 million) and a significant section of Pakistan's manpower is skilled and is fully qualified to adapt to today's technologies.

• Before the founding of Pakistan in 1947, part of the land area that is now Pakistan was one of the main grain-producing centers of the Indian subcontinent under the British Raj,

producing especially wheat.

• Pakistan is the fourth-largest cotton producing nation in the world, behind China, India, and the United States; in 1947 it already had state-of-the-art textile mills and nearly a dozen textile mill equipment manufacturers.

• Unlike the Central Asian nations, it has a major seaport, Karachi, and a long coastline. Through the Arabian Sea, the Persian Gulf, and the Indian Ocean, Pakistan has access to Africa, Southwest and Southeast Asia, and East Asia.

However, over decades, as a result of Pakistan's insufficient and unfocussed leadership, the country was exploited by western nations as a bulwark against the Soviet Union in the Cold war era and later recruited as an "ally" to "fight" the terrorism of Islamic extremists. Islamic extremists and drug traffickers infiltrated the state at almost every level. As a result, Pakistan's economy has stagnated and its social structure has been weakened. China, like many other countries, noticed this development and became concerned.

Pakistan's security problems and its consequent instability also pose a serious threat to China's thinly-populated Xinjiang province, where some Uighur Muslims—not many—have taken up arms against the Chinese authorities under the banner of the Turkistan

CC/Msohaib98

*Karachi, Pakistan's largest city, a port and commercial center on the Arabian Sea.*

Fertile fields in Punjab.

nativepakistan

CPEC highway through a barren region of Balochistan.

Islamic Party or East Turkistan Islamic Movement, seeking a separate nation for the Uighurs. The Uighur jihadis were trained, armed, and sheltered by al-Qaeda, ISIS, and Afghani/Pakistani Taliban, some analysts say. According to Nodirbek Soliev, a specialist in terrorism in China, Russia, and Central Asia, these jihadis—

> have shown their efforts and intentions to strike at China's overseas interests. To meet its growing demand for critical energy and mineral resources, China through its state-owned enterprises has been investing or promised to invest heavily in a number of conflict-affected countries such as Afghanistan, Pakistan, and Iraq.

China also noted that Pakistan's geographical location is a valid reason to engage with the country to achieve success in its One Belt, One Road projects to its west and southwest. It noted that Pakistan has the crucial manpower, an industrial base, food security, and geographical links to China, India, Iran, Afghanistan, and most importantly, is endowed with a long coastline on the Arabian Sea.

China recognized at the outset that just running a transport corridor and building a port would not be sufficient to establish a stable Pakistan. What was required, it envisioned, was to revitalize its decrepit industrial base by building power plants and electricity transmission infrastructure, upgrading its even more decrepit

railroad, and linking its western and southern provinces to the densely populated major production centers of the eastern province of Punjab (see map) with a grid of roads and rails.

## Culture Conflict, Topography, Disunity

The vital importance of such a grid can easily be seen when Pakistan's ethnic divides—corresponding to geographic and topographical differences to a great extent—are considered. Although Pakistan is almost 100 percent Muslim, it suffers from hostility across ethnic and sectarian divides. The sectarian differences include subdivisions within the Sunni (77%) and Shi'a (20%) populations. The ethnic differences correspond to the four major languages—Punjabi, Sindhi, Baloch, and Pashto—which correspond in turn to the four major provinces: Punjab, Sindh, Balochistan, and Khyber-Pakhtunkhwa (KPK), where the people, more often than not, identify themselves by their ethnic and provincial background.

Punjab is agrarian—gifted with rivers and fertile land—and is somewhat similar in its east to the adjacent topography across the border in India.

Sindh, bounded on its south by the Arabian Sea, is desert-like and very short of fresh water.

The two western states, Balochistan and Khyber-Pakhtunkhwa, abut Afghanistan and Iran, and are dominated by two major mountain ranges.

Balochistan is dominated by the Sulaiman Mountains and resembles Zabul province of Afghanistan more than any other part of Pakistan. (It is the bordering region between the Iranian Plateau and the Indian subcontinent, and lies between Iran's Dasht-e-Lut—Lut Desert—and the Indus River that is prominent on the map.) To the north of the Sulaiman Range are the arid highlands of the Hindu Kush, where more than half of the land is above 6,500 feet elevation. The Sulaiman Range, and the high plateau to the west and southwest of it, help to form a natural barrier against moisture-bearing winds that blow in from the Indian Ocean across the Arabian Sea. As a result of this topographical feature, much of Balochistan looks somewhat like the surface of the Moon.

*Neelum Jhelum hydro power project while under construction in Neelum Valley, Azad Kashmir.*

Khyber-Pakhtunkhwa (KPK), north of Balochistan, also borders Afghanistan on the west. The northern areas of KPK are largely mountainous. The Hindu Kush Range to the north begins in Gilgit-Baltistan, moves west into the Chitral District of KPK, and continues into Afghanistan. Immediately south of the Hindu Kush lie three subparallel ranges—Kohistan, Swat, and Dir—which all run north to south and are separated by rivers. Below the mountainous areas of KPK lie the Trans-Indus plains and several minor hill ranges.

The Federally Administered Tribal Areas (FATA)—one of the least accessible regions of Pakistan—lie to the west of Punjab and KPK (see map) in which the Safed Koh Range and the Waziristan Hills form a barrier between Pakistan and Afghanistan.

It is easy to see that in addition to the cultural identities and languages that separate the peoples of the different provinces, the country's topography has so far prevented the integration of the country.

## Power and Transportation

Pakistan is a power-starved nation. With a population close to 185 million, Pakistan's installed electrical power generating capacity is only 21 gigawatts (GW). That is about half of the electric power consumed in Thailand, with a population of about 70 million people. Pakistan's power generation is also highly erratic. During the period of extreme heat in summer, media reports indicate that actual power generation goes down to about 15 GW.

It was evident to China that with such a low power-generation base, developing an economic corridor to stabilize Pakistan would require a large infusion of power production capacity. CPEC has allocated a major part of its funds to power generation and transmission. As of now, projects that would add 10.4 GW of electric power capacity have been started, or are being negotiated. Feasibility studies and negotiations are also on for another 7 GW of power production as part of the CPEC.

The numerous power plants under construction, in negotiation, and being studied for feasibility, include coal-fired, hydro, wind, and solar projects. There is no nuclear component, even though Pakistan has produced nuclear weapons for decades. The CPEC Portal, http://www.cpecinfo.com/, organizes information on these projects and tracks their progress. They are distributed across the four provinces and Pakistan-occupied Kashmir.

The power projects were designed and located to enhance Pakistan's industrial and commercial sectors.

Although some are not on any of the CPEC routes, they are not altogether isolated from them. But the transportation projects were primarily designed to tie in to the CPEC routes or to other roads leading to Gwadar Port.

Among the transport corridor development projects at an advanced stage of completion are these:
- Karakoram Highway Phase II (Havelian-Thakot Section), 120 km
- Karachi-Lahore Motorway (Sukkur-Multan Section), 392 km
- Upgrade of Main Line 1 Railroad (Multan-Lahore Section, 339 km; Hyderabad-Multan Section, 749 km; Kemari-Hyderabad Section, 182 km).

A few other road projects are now under negotiation, including these:
- Khuzdar-Basima Highway (N-30), 110 km
- Karakoram Highway Phase III (Raikot-Thakot Section), 280 km
- D.I. Khan-Quetta Highway (N-50), 533 km.

The CPEC is also developing the area around Gwadar Port. The CPEC Portal notes:

> As part of the China-Pakistan Economic Corridor, and by extension, that of the Silk Route Initiative, Gwadar holds pivotal importance. The port city of Gwadar is a hub of connectivity for the Corridor and an indispensable interchange for the Silk Route… The China-Pakistan Economic Corridor, however, plans not to limit Gwadar to a connecting port only, but enriches it as an economic hub that will cater to the local population by improving their livelihoods. Projects planned for the Gwadar Port City aim at capacitating Balochistan to its full economic, social, technical, and energy potential, and closely integrating it within the economic framework of Pakistan and China.

Among the major projects around the port that have been completed or are under construction—or are about to be launched—the following are of significance:
- Gwadar Eastbay Expressway, 19 km, connecting Gwadar Port to Mehran Coastal Highway
- Gwadar Eastbay Expressway II, 19 km, connecting Eastbay Expressway I to New Gwadar International Airport
- Gwadar New International Airport

- Gwadar Free Zone
- Gwadar Smart Port City Master Plan.

## Enthusiasts and Saboteurs

The successful implementation of the CPEC, and making it secure, could mean a sea-change in the troubled region that includes Afghanistan, Pakistan, and the Indian-administered part of Jammu and Kashmir. A network of economic, trade, and transport connectivity that runs through Pakistan into Afghanistan, Iran, and Central Asia, and is bolstered by China and India, could turn the whole area into a major economic hub. This is recognized by most of the countries that can participate in this network when complete.

Iran has already shown a great deal of interest. Iranian President Hassan Rouhani, in a meeting with Pakistan's Prime Minister, Nawaz Sharif, on the sidelines of the UN General Assembly in September 2016 in New York City, expressed a desire to be part of the CPEC, lauding Prime Minister Sharif's vision that is translating the CPEC into reality. Connectivity projects were recognized by both countries' leaders on that occasion as vital to the progress of the region.

Russia and Afghanistan have also expressed their desire to become a part of the CPEC. The Afghan ambassador to Pakistan, Dr. Omar Zakhilwal, during an interview with Radio Pakistan, said "CPEC is a great project that is equally relevant to Afghanistan, like Pakistan," Pakistan's *Express Tribune* reported, Oct. 15, 2016.

Russia's ambassador to Pakistan, Alexey Y. Dedov, was quoted by India's Times News Network, Dec. 19, 2016, as saying that Russia and Pakistan have held discussions to merge Moscow's Eurasian Economic Union project with the CPEC. Dedov said Russia "strongly" supported CPEC, as it was important for Pakistan's economy and regional connectivity. Some Central Asian countries, such as Tajikistan and Kazakhstan, have made similar endorsements.

The CPEC faces resistance in Balochistan. The corridor's western route, which leads directly to Gwadar Port from Dera Ismail Khan (D.I. Khan on the map), runs through a vast area where insecurity prevails. There are hostile forces, largely based in Balochistan, that openly oppose the construction of the CPEC and are involved in sabotaging efforts to bring in foreign investments and to integrate Balochistan with the rest of the country. Balochistan has been volatile since Pakistan was founded, and some Balochis remain committed to secession. Many years of instability in Afghanistan, which borders Balochistan, and the associated increase of terrorism in the area, have added to the insecurity.

During the construction phase, this insecurity poses a threat to those working on CPEC component projects, especially Chinese workers and technicians. Islamabad is aware of these problems and has assured China that it will provide protection for them. It has also asked Beijing to put in place procedures to maximize the effectiveness of security arrangements by ensuring that Pakistani security officials have prior knowledge of the movement of Chinese personnel in any insecure construction area. Pakistan has established a Special Security Division (SSD) of nine composite infantry battalions (9,000 personnel) and six civilian armed forces wings (6,000 personnel), headed by Major General Abid Rafiq, to provide security for the CPEC throughout the country.

The security issue raised its head again this month. A series of terrorist attacks, although not targeted against the CPEC directly, have rattled Islamabad. ISIS has claimed responsibility for attacks that have killed more than a hundred Pakistanis. It is evident that the efforts of ISIS-backed Wahhabi terrorists are designed to create a situation akin to civil war within Pakistan by targeting the minority Shi'a, the Sufis, and other Islamic sects.

**Protect Domestic Manufactures**

In addition to security concerns, Pakistan's small and medium-size industries have expressed fears that they may come under pressure because of cheaper and plentiful imports from China further facilitated by the fully operational CPEC. In November 2016, Pakistan's news daily, the *Express Tribune*, quoted Atif Iqbal, Executive Director of the Organization for Advancement and Safeguard of Industrial Sector, who pointed out that the Free Trade Agreement with China has not been favorable to Pakistan. "It is imperative for the government of Pakistan to keep in mind all these factors while negotiating the second phase of the FTA with China," he said. He is of the view that in talks with China, some leverage should be provided for Pakistan's products, to enable local industry to compete.

*An earlier report on the CPEC by Ramtanu Maitra, titled, "China-Pakistan Economic Corridor: The Challenges," was published in* EIR *on April 15, 2016.*

# Minds that Soar Above the Impossible

by Marsha Freeman and Dennis Speed

*The following is Part 2 of a review of both the current film* Hidden Figures *as well as the book* Hidden Figures: the American Dream and the Untold Story of the Black Women Mathematicians Who Helped Win the Space Race *by Margot Lee Shetterly. For Part 1, see* our previous issue.

Feb 21—In 1987, economist Lyndon LaRouche, a candidate for the 1988 Presidency, wrote and released a thirty-minute television treatment called *The Woman On Mars*. Its title paid tribute to a 1929 film made by director Fritz Lang, *The Woman In The Moon*. It was a forty-year perspective for a possible direction for the United States space program. It was unique in the Presidential race of that year, and every year since.

*Not all civil rights marches took place in front of the cameras. In this scene from* Hidden Figures, *Dorothy Vaughan's "West computers" transfer to new quarters to become an integral part of the new space program.*

The idea of *The Woman On Mars* or *The Woman In The Moon* turns out to have been not so unique as it has appeared to us in the past. That is the particularly useful feature of the recent movie, *Hidden Figures.* There is a little known story of intellectual courage at the very center of the United States space program that is now receiving merited attention.

When John Glenn stepped into his Mercury capsule in February 1962, sitting atop an Atlas Intercontinental Ballistic Missile, he undoubtedly recalled the very first test launch of an Atlas that the seven Mercury astronauts had witnessed—the rocket blew up in front of their eyes.

Many acts of courage, however, take place, not on television, but outside of public view, often with few or no witnesses, never to be acknowledged. These acts are often the most important in enabling the leaps a society makes in conquering its most daunting challenges. The black women "West Computers," as portrayed in the film *Hidden Figures,* and the women in the NASA program as a whole, had no lesser role to play in putting Americans into space and the first man on the Moon, than the astronauts whose lives depended upon them. Their courage was grounded in their brilliant minds, their self confidence, and their determination that the "social order" could be challenged, through what they could accomplish.

That courage, however, did not come from them as mere individuals. There was a social and institutional tradition of excellence out of which they "sprang." It had been invented in Lincoln's and Grant's America by post-slavery African-Americans and their non-Black allies in such organizations as the American Missionary Association. This educational movement, unacknowledged but fundamental to American intellectual life, starting in 1866 and extending unbroken through the 1930s, fostered that mental toughness, creativity and resilience. It was rooted in the Grant-era Reconstruction and post-Reconstruction southern educational system's Hampton, Tuskegee, Fisk, Rust, and 490 other schools and Historically Black Colleges and Universities (HCBUs) that were created over the eighty years prior to *Hidden Figures'* area of concentration. In fact, Margot Shetterly's companion book, *Hidden Figures: the American Dream and the Untold Story of the Black Women Mathematicians Who Helped Win the Space Race* is, in its own way, as much a resurrection of the importance of these institutions as it is a re-discovery of the "human computers" upon whom it concentrates.

For example, author Shetterly usefully provides the background story of one of those women, the now-famous and NASA-celebrated Katherine Goebel Johnson, thus:

> In 1933,Katherine entered West Virginia State College as a fifteen-year old freshman.... The school's formidable president, Dr. John W. Davis, was, like W.E.B. DuBois and Booker T. Washington, part of the exclusive fraternity of "race men," Negro educators, and public intellectuals who set the debate over the best course of progress for black America ... James C. Evans, an MIT engineering graduate, ran the school's trade and mechanical studies program before accepting a position as a Civilian Aide in the War Department in 1942.

These and other wartime connections provided the conveyor-belt for qualified African-Americans, who had actually always been available, to serve their country at levels above the expectations of the institutions into which they were introduced. As Tuskegee Airman pilot instructor Daniel "Chappie" James, later to become the nation's first African-American four-star general, said, "My mother used to say: 'Don't stand there banging on the door to opportunity, then, when someone opens it, you say, 'Wait a minute, I got to get my bags.' You be prepared with your bags of knowledge, your patriotism, your honor, and when somebody opens the door, you charge in.'"

Of one of Katherine Johnson's teachers, Shetterly tells us:

> On staff in the math department was William Waldron Schieffelin Claytor... Just twenty-seven years old, Claytor played Rachmaninoff with finesse and a mean game of tennis. He drove a sports car and piloted his own plane. Claytor's brusque manner intimidated most of his students, who couldn't keep up as the professor furiously scribbled mathematical formulas on the chalk board with one hand and just as quickly erased them with the other. He moved from one topic to the next, making no concession to their bewildered expressions. But Katherine, serious and bespectacled with fine curly hair, made such quick work of the course catalog that Clayton had to create advanced classes just for her.

Despite the fact that there was no apparent possibility for "career advancement" for an African-American woman in the sciences, Claytor insisted that he was preparing Katherine for a career in research, a career that did not yet exist! The space program, precisely because it was based on creating that which did not exist, was precisely where Katherine Johnson would find herself, because she *could* find herself there. She had been prepared for the future, which one can forecast, but not directly see, and space research was that future.

## Kennedy's Apollo Project Creates the Future

When President John F. Kennedy announced that the United States would land a man on the Moon by the end of the 1960s, the leisurely pace of NASA's manned Mercury program was replaced with the all-out national drive to meet the President's deadline. New facilities, to train astronauts, build a new Statue-of-Liberty-sized rocket, run the test stand and wind tunnel tests to make sure it would fly, and develop the men and materiel to carry out the mandate, had to be created. The National Advisory Committee on Aeronautics (NACA) already had research and development and test facilities, in California, Ohio, and Virginia. They would be absorbed into NASA, which would add rocket research to the menu of their responsibilities.

These NACA centers could have been expanded to take on the new responsibilities of manned missions, but the leadership of the space agency sought instead to create new facilities. These, it would site in Alabama, Mississippi, Texas, Louisiana, and Florida. President Kennedy and the leadership of NASA saw the space program as a vehicle toward integration in the South.

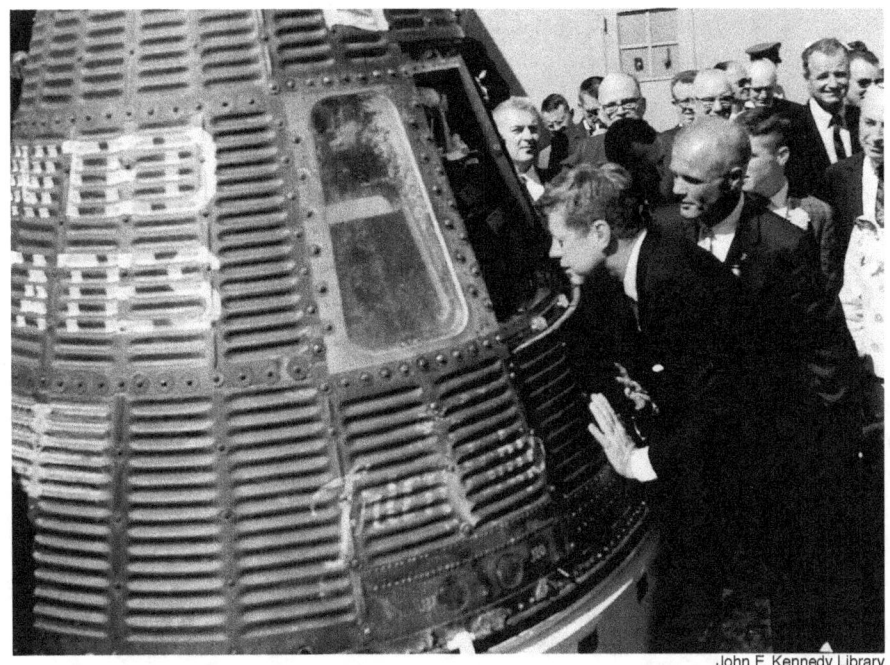

President John Kennedy inspecting the interior of Friendship 7 with John Glenn. Sending the first American into Earth orbit required the insight to "see beyond the numbers," and invent a new mathematics. Astronaut John Glenn did not step into his Friendship 7 capsule until he had been assured that "human computer" Katherine Johnson had "checked the numbers."

*John F. Kennedy Library*

King, Jr. was incarcerated in the city jail, writing his "Letter," now one of the most famous documents in American history. That movement had successfully integrated Birmingham stores and had defeated the infamous racist police chief, Eugene "Bull" Connor, after Kennedy's White House had been made aware, including by the statements of world leaders, of the outrage registered in many countries at the pictures of police dogs, water-hosing, and the incarceration of seven-year olds.

In that speech, Kennedy asserted the principle of the sovereign authority of the Federal Government—through the policy of public improvements to promote the General Welfare of the nation as a whole—to be identical with the guarantee of the right to develop to all its citizens, regardless of circumstance or ethnicity. Kennedy said that the Tennessee Valley Authority

In all of these states, racial segregation was the law. Between 1882 and 1968, Mississippi led the nation in black lynchings, with five hundred thirty-nine that have been documented. Just in the years of Franklin Roosevelt's Presidency, between 1933 and 1945, there were one hundred black lynchings in the South. But President Kennedy believed that "a rising tide lifts all boats," and that venturing out into "this new ocean of space," would open opportunities for the nation's disenfranchised. Shortly after taking office, the President issued an Executive Order requiring federal agencies to hire minorities, and at the time, NASA was the fastest growing federal agency in the deep South.

Two years later, in Muscle Shoals, Alabama, during a celebration of the thirtieth anniversary of Franklin Roosevelt's Tennessee Valley Authority, sitting beside President Kennedy on the platform was Alabama Governor George Wallace, who, in his inaugural speech four months earlier, had declared: "Segregation now, segregation tomorrow, segregation forever." This was on May 18, just thirteen days after Wallace's defeat by the civil rights' Children's Crusade in Birmingham, initiated by the Rev. James Bevel while Martin Luther

stands for cooperation between public and private enterprise, between upstream and downstream interests, between those who are concerned with power and navigation, flood control and recreation, and above all, cooperation between the Federal Government and the seven states of this area... From time to time statements are made labeling the Federal Government an outsider, an intruder, an adversary. In any free federation of States, of course differences will arise and difficulties will persist. But the people of this area know that the United States Government is not a stranger or not an enemy. It is the people of the fifty states joining in a national effort to see progress in every state of the Union.

Progress, social progress through economic and technological progress, was the first and foremost reliable force for national unity. The public civil rights movement would put a national spotlight on racial discrimination in this country, and the violent opposition to equal rights. Yet, there was something else: a national vision and sense of purpose, held by those at NASA, which would over time overwhelm all else in the service of its accomplishment. *Hidden Figures* and its companion book provide a more thorough description than is otherwise available, of that cultural shift in America, of its unbridled technological optimism. It was an intellectual "human rights movement"— the right to be creative on the very frontier of all human scientific knowledge—that these women scientists led, not through marching (though some did that as well), but by means of their accomplishments, a necessary and welcome complement to those marches.

Asked in an interview last December, carried by *inverse.com,* whether she thought the women in her history "saw a connection between their own work and the advancement of civil rights," author Margot Shetterly replied, "Absolutely, there's no question. They saw a very direct result. Their attitude was, 'We're here, we are doing this work, and we are helping our country advance because we are also opening the door for people like us.'" She continued, "They realized that everything they did would have an implication for future women."

**The Next Generation**

*Hidden Figures* provides an opportunity, unlike Hollywood "special effects space movies" like "Gravity," not only to acquaint two generations of Americans with the real heroes still in their midst, but to galvanize today's United States past the desert of the Obama years—back into space.

On Jan. 7, Katherine Johnson's great-grandson, University of Guam student Trevor Boykin, hosted a special screening of *Hidden Figures,* at the Micronesian Mall Theater. His purpose was to honor his now-famous great-grandmother, and to generate funds from the proceeds to go toward a Science, Technology, Engineering, and Mathematics (STEM) scholarship in her name. The event raised about $1,000,000, and the two hundred in attendance were education officials and students of all ages.

NASA has sponsored a series of events to bring this previously unpublicized space history to the public. On Dec. 1, NASA kicked off what will be a year-long centennial celebration of the Langley Research Center, the real-life location of the events portrayed in *Hidden Figures.* An educational event, led by Administrator Charlie Bolden, included Octavia Spencer, who plays mathematician Dorothy Vaughan (and has been nominated for an Academy Award) in the film.

On Dec. 12, the Kennedy Space Center held a news conference with cast members from the film, which was shown live on NASA TV and the agency's website. In January, after the film's official release, NASA's Glenn Research Center and Cuyahoga Community College took three hundred fifty students from fourteen local schools to see the film. After the movie, the students had the opportunity to participate in some science-related activities and hear from space professionals, including Dr. Christine Darden, retired from NASA. Darden worked in the same computing department depicted in *Hidden Figures.* She said, "We never know how many people we impact in the audience, but when I retired from NASA there were two female engineers that said I was the reason why they were there."

The actresses in the film, who, like most other Americans, knew nothing of the characters they would portray, and just as little about the space program overall before they read the script, were transformed into promoters of space exploration as they learned that history, and met the people who made it. They have taken up the cause of bringing this proud history to as wide an audience as possible. All of them have participated in round-table discussions, press conferences, movie premiers, and other public activities to promote the film. Octavia Spencer bought out the tickets at a local cinema in Los Angeles over the Martin Luther King Day weekend in January, to enable single parents to bring their children to see the film. "If you know a family in need that would like to see our movie but can't afford it, have them come… My mom would not have been able to afford to take me and my siblings. So, I'm honoring her and all single parents this weekend."

NASA itself had previously recognized the contributions of the "West Computers." Katherine Johnson, the principal "computer" in Margot Shetterly's book, had received special NASA achievement awards in 1970, 1980, and 1985. Yet, in an interview on "Quora," published by *Forbes* on Feb. 9, Robert Frost, NASA instructor and flight controller, was asked if current space agency employees were aware of the women portrayed in the *Hidden Figures* film. Frost stated that people who were "not aware, were not paying attention." Referring to Johnson, Frost said, "Katherine got a lot of attention nine years ago, when she was profiled on the main NASA website. I first learned about her about fifteen years ago when a manuscript called 'Human Computers: The Women in Aeronautical Research,' by a Beverly Golemba, was discussed at a staff meeting."

Therefore, it is the film that has reached millions of people across the country and around the world. (*Hidden Figures* did surpass the *Star Wars* prequel at the box office on the first weekend of its release.) The movie is, however, transient. Margot Shetterly's book is a more durable inspiration and contribution, which should be studied by all American youth twelve years old and up, as well as adults.

NASA

*Engineer, medical doctor and astronaut Mae Jemison, became the first African-American woman in space during her 1992 mission on the Space Shuttle Endeavour. Since leaving NASA she has actively encouraged young women to make their mark in history—in science, technology, and engineering.*

## Our Historic Moment

What our nation needs is a full re-commitment to the vision of Kennedy, Glenn, Yuri Gagarin, Sergei Korolyov, and the hundreds of thousands of persons who carried out the greatest voyage in human history, to change our identity as a human species. China's commitment to return to the Moon, to its currently completely unexplored far side; the possibility of mining helium-3 on the Moon as a source for thermonuclear fusion technology; the creation of interplanetary telescopes to peer more fully into deep space; the "space medicine" breakthroughs that promise the extension of human life; and the exploration of the other planets—this is the future that is truly intended for mankind. Why has the United States retreated from the vision of the future that inspired our greatest contribution to science?

The true "hidden figure" of our time is the creative mind of the human race, hidden from itself by the continued dominance of the infantile culture of war and the foolish acquisition of what is believed to be wealth—wealth which can be redefined and generated in a uniquely new form with every fundamental technologi-

cal breakthrough by the human mind. Wealth and resources are not pre-existent, but are created by the human mind. Hampton Institute's, and other schools' students of the 1940s and 1950s, knew that they were free in their minds, and therefore rich, not poor—no matter how "hidden" they might seem to be. It is space exploration that can provide the same experience of freedom to all of the American people, if it is now resumed as the "science driver" of a new era in human self-development.

The American poet and scientist Edgar Poe warned us that should we seek Eldorado, we must travel "over the mountains of the Moon." Poe knew more than the economists and financial predators of today, who tell us that "space is too expensive." The only thing that the exploration of space costs us, is that we have to give up our much-valued stupidity, whether about the non-existent idea of "race," or of "territorial rights," or of "human overpopulation." If sixty million Chinese school children can watch Chinese scientists discuss weightlessness from space, why can't the same number of American children be introduced to a new Chinese-Russian-American-Indian-international space project now, using the opportunity of a new Administration that has not said "No" to man's future?

# The Space Program Is Key to Organizing The Best Talents of Our Nation

by Kesha Rogers

*We choose to go to the Moon. We choose to go to the Moon in this decade and do the other things, not because they are easy, but because they are hard, because that goal will serve to organize and measure the best of our energies and skills, because that challenge is one that we are willing to accept, one we are unwilling to postpone, and one which we intend to win, and the others, too.*

*— President John F. Kennedy*

Feb. 21—Monday, February 20 marked the 55th Anniversary of the day that the first American orbited the Earth. On February 20, 1962, John Glenn rocketed into space aboard the Project Mercury capsule, Friendship 7. Glenn circled the globe three times in four hours and fifty-six minutes.

Now we reflect on the importance of that day in history, and on John Glenn's contribution to implementing the vision and challenge to the nation put forth by President John F. Kennedy, "to land a man on the Moon and return him safely to Earth" before that decade, the 1960s, was out. His challenge to the nation came only a few weeks after the famous flight of astronaut Alan Shepard, the first American to make a suborbital flight into space, a flight of less than 16 minutes on May 5, 1961. These missions were televised. The accomplishments of our nation's space program inspired our entire nation and the world, and inspired a deter-

NASA

*At Cape Canaveral, Dr. Wernher von Braun explains the Saturn Launch System to President Kennedy, Nov. 16, 1963.*

mination in President Kennedy to commit the nation to the greater mission. We would be first to the Moon, but our mission would not stop there.

The success of John Glenn's flight 55 years ago, and the achievements of other American astronauts and Soviet cosmonauts—such as Yuri Gagarin, the first person to orbit the Earth—proved that there are no limits to what mankind can accomplish, that there is nothing that can hold us back, including the ostensibly budget-driven policies that we are seeing today. And so the nation was determined that Kennedy had laid out a mission and that, despite all odds, it was one we would accomplish. On July 20, 1969, Americans would be the first human beings to set foot on the Moon and "come in peace for all mankind." The goal was only met by doing as President Kennedy would declare, by organizing the best energies and skills of our nation.

That is the outlook and understanding required today, to restore a national mission and once again inspire great optimism in the people of this nation and the world. We need strong determination to continue to reach for new frontiers in the exploration and development of space. We need a vision for the nation, for our young people, not the endless funding of imperial wars and bailing out of Wall Street speculators. As astronaut John Glenn once said,

The most important thing we can do is inspire young minds and to advance the kind of science, math, and technology education that will help youngsters take us to the next phase of space travel.

## Fight Wall Street, Defend the Mind

President Trump has promised to establish a national mission to relaunch our space program. That requires us to unify the nation and the world around the kind of win-win cooperation that has been offered by China. We must commit to working with China and Russia, to continue the mapping of the lunar surface, and to work on constructing stations there: The lunar surface continues to be the gateway to the Solar System, the gateway to Mars.

We must put an end to the hypocrisy, the sabotage, the destructive policies that are coming from the Wall Street apparatus in the U.S. Congress that says we cannot work with China.

We must also stop the sabotage coming from the Wall Street apparatus of former President Barack Obama, who is actually putting in place more policies to create division and destruction in the nation, as he did when, as President, he cancelled the Constellation program for manned spaceflight to the Moon by 2020 and then to Mars. His efforts to set our space program back have continued since his departure from the Presidency.

Even in a Feb. 16 Congressional hearing of the Committee on Science, Space, and Technology, titled, "NASA: Past Present and Future," certain members continued to push insane, monetarist ideas that continue to sabotage our nation's commitment to space exploration. There were questions such as, "How do we stop the increase in the budget of our space program?" "How do you establish responsible stewardship of the American taxpayer's dollar?" "Don't we need public/private partnerships to augment taxpayers' investments?"

Congress should be more concerned about, "How do we stop the continuing wars, costing billions and trillions of dollars, to support terrorism, to defend ISIS?" and "How do we stop the trillion-dollar bailouts on behalf of Wall Street derivatives?" These have to be stopped! There is no excuse whatsoever for taking the future away from our young people. The space program and NASA are key to the scientific and economic progress of the nation. They develop the talents and skills of our nation!

## It's Not the Money, Stupid!

China has lifted more than 700 million people out of the most dire poverty. How did it do that? China's leadership had a vision for their nation, for their future, for their young people. They have committed their nation to being the first to land on the far side of the Moon. They are organizing nations around the world to cooperate in establishing a permanent presence on the Moon. The United States must join in such a mission. We must inspire a new generation of young scientists, astronauts, and engineers. During the Feb. 16 Congressional hearing, former astronaut Harrison Schmitt stated that our space program needs a generation of leaders with an average age of 30 or less, because young people are not afraid of risk, they're not afraid of taking on new challenges and responsibilities.

People are now too concerned about "my money." We need to be concerned about the future and the development of our people. We must be concerned about inspiring every person in our society to be creative and productive. It was not "the money" that launched our nation to the Moon. It was vision and creativity. Today Margot Shetterly's book, *Hidden Figures*, and the movie based on it, remind us of that (see review, p.29).

Some of the greatest, little known pioneers in the space program were engineers and mathematicians behind the scenes, including a very brilliant, creative group of African American women who were "computers," mathematicians, and engineers. Katherine Johnson was a member of that talented African American group, and John Glenn made sure that *she* checked the calculations of the machine before he would travel into space.

He was not concerned about whether a machine could do the job; he trusted the power of the human mind. If John Glenn had not made that trip, would we have landed on the Moon? Would we have accomplished the goal that President Kennedy set out? Was it the machine or the mind that got us there?

It's time to rid the nation of our commitment to monetarism. It should never have been allowed to dominate this country. We must go back to the understanding that economic value is based on the creative powers of the human mind. Our space program is the key to advancing the economy of our nation and of the world. Cooperation is key.

Many members of Congress in office today were inspired by the space program under President Kennedy. Now, they sit there and say, "Well, we can't do it, because we can't afford it." That's insanity, that is sabotage, and it has to be stopped.

We must put our space program, NASA, and cooperation with many nations around the world back at the top of our nation's agenda.

# Musical Dialogue-of-Culture Concert Breakthrough in Copenhagen

by Michelle Rasmussen

COPENHAGEN, Feb. 17—They came from around the world this evening. They came bearing gifts. Not gifts you could touch with your hands. But gifts that touched your soul. Gifts of beautiful music, and beautiful dance.

And the people came to hear them. And they kept coming, and they kept coming till all of the 120 seats were taken. And after there was no more room for extra chairs, they stood in the aisles, and they stood in the lobby, and they sat behind the curtains. They were Danes, and they were diplomats and other people from many nations, maybe 180-200 people in total. The hostess said that there had never been so many there before.

Bai Claire Jie
*Indonesian traditional dancer, Sarah Noor Komarudin, performing a Jaipong dance.*

Bai Claire Jie
*Soloist Valery Likhachev*

Bai Claire Jie
*Soloist Leena Malkki*

*The* Svetit Mesyats *[The Moon is Shining] ensemble from the Russian House, conducted by Igor Panich.*

*Gitta-Maria Sjöberg, recently retired from the royal Danish Opera.*

Bai Claire Jie

*Kai Guo, from Mongolia with Feride Istogu Gillesberg.*

The dialogue of cultures between the sponsors of the concert, itself, led to the great success: the Schiller Institute, the Russian-Danish Dialogue organization, the Russian House in Copenhagen, and the China Culture Center of the Chinese Embassy (about to open, which also provided food during the intermission). And the concert was held in the Russian Center for Science and Culture, tied to the Russian Embassy, representing the Russian Federation's authority for connection to the CIS countries (of the former Soviet Union), Russians living abroad, and international humanistic cooperation (*Rossotrudnichestvo*).

First, the people were told by Schiller Institute chairman Tom Gillesberg that we have

Kristian von Späth

*Fred (left) and Isaac Kwaku, from Ghana.*

a unique moment in world history, where the potential is there for the United States to join the new paradigm of economic development sweeping the world. Then they were told by the spokeswoman for the Russian-Danish Dialogue, Jelena Nielsen, that a dialogue of culture can lead to peace in the world. These two were also the alternating hosts for the evening. Finally, the director of the Russian Center for Science and Culture, Artem Alexandrovich Markaryan, welcomed the people. Then the procession of gift-givers began.

From Russia came the *Svetit Mesyats* [The Moon is Shining] ensemble from the Russian House, conducted by Igor Panich. These were children playing Russian folk songs on balalaikas, including "Katyusha," with soloist Valery Likhachev, baritone, who has sung on 200 stages. He also later performed Leporello's "List"

aria, from the opera *Don Giovanni* by Mozart, and Mephistopheles' couplets, from Gounod's opera *Faust*, together with his pianist Semyon Bolshem.

From China's Mongolia came a very musical young science student, Kai Guo, who played many flutes, and he and Feride Istogu Gillesberg from the Schiller Institute, charmingly sang the "Kangding" Chinese love song, as a duet.

From Indonesia came a traditional dancer, Sarah Noor Komarudin, who filled the room with her graceful Jaipong dance.

From Ghana came two young men, Isaac Kwaku and Fred Kwaku, who sang and played a religious song, and a song depicting the point that when we work together, we are stronger than when we stand alone.

And from Denmark and Sweden came three out-

*Pianist Benjamin Telmányi and his mother, Anika, played Beethoven's Romance for Violin and Piano, Op. 50.*

Bai Claire Jie

*Soloist Idil Alpsoy, a member of the Middle East Peace Orchestra.*

standing female opera singers, whose tones and dramatic intensity, moved the audience profoundly. Their offerings were songs and arias from Schubert, Verdi, Dvořák, and Sibelius. Gitta-Maria Sjöberg, an international bright star of a soprano who recently retired from the Royal Danish Opera, sang "Rusalka's Song to the Moon" by Dvořák. Idil Alpsoy, a fantastic mezzo soprano with roots in Hungary and Turkey, who is also a member of the Middle East Peace Orchestra, sang songs from Sibelius' Op. 37 and 88. And a soprano, Leena Malkki, whom we have heard for many years blossoming into a truly magnificent artist, sang Schubert's "Gretchen am Spinnrade" (spinning wheel), and Desdemona's prayer *Ave Maria,* from Verdi's opera *Othello.* The first two (Sjöberg and Alpsoy) were accompanied by Christine Raft, an extremely talented young Danish pianist, and the latter (Malkki) by the Schiller Institute's own Benjamin Telmányi Lylloff.

He and his mother Anika, poignantly played Beethoven's "Romance for Violin and Piano," Op. 50, continuing the legacy bequeathed by their ancestor from Hungary, the violin soloist Emil Telmányi Lylloff.

For the finale, all the singers (but one), sang Verdi's chorus of the Hebrew slaves longing for freedom, "Và, pensiero," with the addition of four members of the Schiller Institute's future chorus. See the program at: http://schillerinstitut.dk/si/?p=17965 Video and audio will also be posted to this link.

And the audience was uplifted, with each presentation by itself, and with the succession of one piece of music, or dance, after the other, one country after another—traditional music in dialogue with classical music, weaving a tapestry of sound, sight, and delight, not reaching their senses, but their soul.

As they left, they all expressed the most sublime joy and thankfulness for having had the privilege to have received all of these precious gifts, which they took home in the memory of their minds, to be opened again, and again.

A musical testament to the paradox of the unity and diversity of mankind, expressed by human creativity, and a powerful statement of the dialogue of cultures was declaimed.

We will go forth with this statement, in the form of professional video and audio recordings, to spread its ripples throughout the world.

*For the Finale, all the singers and members of the Schiller Institute Chorus sang "Va Pensiero," Verdi's chorus of the Hebrew slaves longing for freedom.*

# III. LaRouche in 1998

# The Substance of Morality[1]

by Lyndon H. LaRouche, Jr.

May 28, 1998

Evidence from as early as hundreds of thousands of years ago, shows the continuing existence of hominids capable of those kinds of discovery of physical principle, the which place mankind apart from, and absolutely above the higher apes.[2] All competent scientific inquiry respecting the nature of the human species, and of qualities specific to human behavior, rests upon a showing of crucial evidence of our species' distinguishing, manifest type of generation of an original or replicated discovery of a physical principle. No substitute for such knowledge of principles exists among outgrowths of such qualitatively inferior levels of mental activity as deduction or mere animal "learning from repeatable experience."

On this point, the combined archeological and historical record shows, that the totality of human existence,[3] as a developing, functional fraction of the totality of our growing biosphere,[4] is dominated by an accumulation of progress in increase of mankind's power over nature, a measurement conveniently reflected upon our perceptual apparatus in the form of increase of demographic values, per capita and per square kilometer, of the Earth's surface. The human species is unique in its capacity for willful changes of this sort in its relationship, both to the biosphere and the universe in general.

Yet, in these facts lies a relevant, crucial paradox. The human species' long-term progress, when measured, as a whole, over the span of hundreds of generations, shows progress to be a crucial, characteristic, and implicitly inevitable feature of our species, as a species. However, it is not simply pre-assured that every step of progress during a shorter term, such as several or more generations of a global or local culture, will lead to its appropriate supercessor. Scientific and technological progess, as such, are indispensable for the continued progress of the entirety of our species. However, when and whether progress, or even retrogression occurs, is never automatic; the actual outcome is a result of what we term "cultural factors," as much as impulses attributable to progress in discovery of higher physical principles as such.

In fact, for reasons to be considered here, it is "cultural factors" which govern even scientific and technological progress as such, and which also govern the manner in which discovered physical principles are fostered and realized in ways bearing upon improvements in both man's physical power over nature, and the realization of that physical power in the form of net improvements in demographic characteristics of cultures.

Presently, the ongoing, global financial and monetary collapse, has been plunging the once-proud civili-

---

1. See, the references to the relationship between an "m-fold" and "n-fold" manifold, in Lyndon H. LaRouche, Jr., "Russia Is Eurasia's Keystone Economy," prologue to report by Dr. Sergei Glazyev, **Executive Intelligence Review**, March 27, 1998, pp. 45-51.

2. Recent archaeological work in Germany has revealed well-crafted throwing spears, solidly dated to about 400,000 years ago. The use of such technology predating 40,000 years ago was previously unknown. The wooden spears were shaped and balanced to be used as javelins, rather than simple thrusting implements, and reflect a technological skill by their makers, that has generally not been credited to humans of this Pleistocene, so-called Lower Paleolithic, period. See Hartmut Thieme, "Lower Paleolithic Hunting Spears from Germany," **Nature**, Feb. 27, 1997, pp. 807-810; Robin Dennell, "The World's Oldest Spears," Feb. 27, 1997, pp. 767-768.

3. I.e., as a component of the existence and development of the biosphere as a whole.

4. Man is part of the total biosphere. Man's portion of the biosphere increases, but the biosphere also grows, per capita. Compare this with Vernadsky's conception of a noösphere.

EIRNS/Chris Lewis

*Schiller Institute musicians rehearse for a performance of Bach's St. John's Passion on April 4, 1998, at the St. Margaretha Roman Catholic Church in Ampfing, Germany. "Our task here," LaRouche writes, "is to lead the reader into a breakthrough in recognizing, from the example of music, the nature of the* ontological *principle involved in Classical culture, as a whole."*

and, for the U.S.A., Benjamin Franklin's great-grandson, the Humboldt-linked Alexander Dallas Bache.[6]

On this account, generally speaking, when compared to the superior levels of culture represented by early to middle Nineteenth-Century European Classical culture in general, even the leading sections of those of today's populations dominated by our recent generations of global, European-dominated trends in global cultures, are ignorant, appallingly backward, even relatively bestial. [See box on the next page.] This recent, moral and cultural degeneration of successive post-World War II generations, is typified by the recent rise in homicidal outbreaks of existentialism among present-day adolescents.[7] This deplorable trend is typical of the ma-

zation of the 1946-1963 post-war reconstruction period, into the threatened onset of a world-wide "new dark age." We are faced, thus, once again, with the fact, that the most powerful technological cultures can be doomed by the kind of moral and cultural "paradigm shift" which has dominated the world, increasingly, since the 1964-1972 youth-counterculture revolt against both technological progress and rationality generally.

Therefore, sane national and related policies depend upon discovering and adopting those principles of culture to which we must turn, if we are to avert the seemingly inevitable demographic and per-capita collapse now gripping this planetary civilization. The author proposes, that the nature and importance of such cultural issues, ought to have been made clear by those studies of the principles of Classical art-forms and education which had occupied the best minds of the scientists, artists, and statesmen of European civilization's early Nineteenth Century, such as, for Germany, Friedrich Schiller and his friends, the brothers von Humboldt,[5]

5. Marianna Wertz, "The Classical Curriculum of Wilhelm von Humboldt," **Fidelio**, Summer 1996, pp. 29-39.

6. Alexander Dallas Bache (1806-1867) graduated U.S. Military Academy (1825); was sent to Europe in 1836 to work with scientists and educational leaders including Carl F. Gauss, Wilhelm Weber, and Alexander von Humboldt. Bache formed an elite American grouping of scientists, cooperating with German and French co-thinkers. He and his aides designed and organized the U.S. Naval Academy. As chief of the U.S. Coast and Geodetic Survey, Bache was chief strategist for the emergence of an advanced U.S. military-industrial capability, and the creation of the electrical industry; he was a leading intelligence adviser to President Abraham Lincoln.

7. Six serious incidents of school killings have taken place in rural areas of America since February 1996, involving children between the ages of 11 and 16. In two cases, the children killed their parents, before proceeding to the schools, where they also killed classmates and teachers. In all cases, the children were immersed in video games, such as "Mortal Kombat," mind-numbing rock music, and violent films. Note, that in five of the cases, the children are being tried as adults.
The phenomenon of juvenile violence in Germany was addressed by Countess Marion Dönhoff, in an editorial in the weekly **Die Zeit** on April 8, 1998. Titled "These Are Our Children," she points to such sources of juvenile violence as "the lack of sense of injustice, intolerance, extreme ego-centrism"—the results of a permissive society in which "everything revolves around material and commercial success." Such cultural degeneration is an example of what Nazi existentialist

# The Humboldt Curriculum

*Wilhelm von Humboldt (1767-1835) was director of ecclesiastical affairs and education in Prussia from 1809 to 1810, giving him—for the brief span of about a year—responsibility for all public cultural and scientific institutions. During this time, he transformed Prussian education, with far-reaching effects for generations to come. This description of his program is taken from an article by Helga Zepp-LaRouche, "The Modernity of the Humboldtian Education Ideal."*

In the two documents he wrote on the educational system of Königsberg and Lithuania, Humboldt lays out what he thinks to be the "aim of education" the formal shaping *Bildung* of the entire man into a harmonious totality.

"Each individual, even the poorest, receives a complete education as man, each one absolutely completely, only where he might continue to make further progress; those who may have certain limitations also find their right and their place, and no one should have to set a goal sooner than in his own gradual development; after all, most of them will still have to, even after leaving school, make a transition from merely being taught, to further development in specialist institutions."

Humboldt was very much opposed to any form of mere career-oriented drill, which he saw practiced in the cadet institutions and the vocational schools; indeed, he even warned that a "merely drilled man should always be useless and dangerous."

Formally, Humboldt's concept has the three phases of schooling—elementary, *gymnasium* (secondary school), and university—upon one another, each complementing the other. Humboldt emphasized that the teaching of philology, mathematics, and history are of equal importance. A plan of studies designed according to his proposals, envisaged for the *Sexta* [about the first year of secondary school—the student would be about 13 years old] had the following ordering: 12 hours language instruction (Latin and German), 13 hours scientific subjects (Mathematics 6, science 2, geography 3, religion 2), 3 hours of drawing, 4 hours of calligraphy, and additionally, singing and gymnastics.

For the *Prima* [the last year of high school before entering university] the following hours were envisaged: 8 Latin, 7 Greek, 4 German, 6 Mathematics, 2 science, 3 history and geology, 2 religion. For the first time, Greek (Plato, Homer, Sophocles) was read from the *Quarta* [equivalent to about 8th or 9th grade] until the *Prima*.

In designing this curriculum] for the *Gymnasium*, Humboldt defined two centers of gravity: the teaching of the ideal concept of man embodied in the Greek Classics, and the teaching of Philology, which two were for Humboldt the nucleus of philosophy, history, and mathematics.

At the University, there should be only researchers: those who are autonomous, and those guided by others, through which the unity of teaching and research should also be preserved—Humboldt wished that it might bring forth the "deepest and purest aspect of knowledge/science *Wissenschaft*." Knowledge from whose organic unity he proceeded as a basic principle, must be built upon a principle, it must not consist of an accidental collection of facts.

Because of the fortunate circumstance that Humboldt became responsible for the Prussian education system at its most decisive moment, the ideal of man, oriented towards the Greek Classics was of decisive influence for more than a Century for the intellectual elite who received their education at a humanistic *gymnasium*.

## Humboldt in America

*The Humboldt Classical humanist curriculum was used as a model for U.S. high schools, thanks to the efforts of Benjamin Franklin's great-grandson Alexander Dallas Bache, as Anton Chaitkin reports:*

Alexander Dallas Bache travelled in Europe (1836-38), examining 280 schools in the British Isles, Germany, Austria, France, Italy, and other countries. His detailed report on his educational findings is a milestone in the history of American schools.

Bache was the first president of Philadelphia's Central High, the first U.S. public high school outside New England, and the model for successful American urban schools. Bach was said to have organized Central High School, in particular, on the principles of the *Gymnasium* and *Real* schools of the Leipzig system. He created a pioneering laboratory for measurement of the Earth's magnetism, employing his students as the observers, and he equipped Central High with one of the world's finest astronomical observatories, with the students under the supervision of the leading astronomers of the era.

jority of both the top-most ranks, and the lower levels of today's society.

The challenge of reversing the present cultural and physical-economic collapse of global civilization, is the context for the following report. The solution to the difficulties of comprehending these presently most urgent matters, was first discovered, and, later, developed in the following way.

## 1. Three Crucial Discoveries

It was during the interval 1948-1952, that I first made three original, interdependent discoveries of physical principle, a set of principles whose continued and interconnected development has since dominated my life, my professional and related accomplishments, and also the controversies in which I have become an increasing central figure of recent decades.

The first among these principles, is one whose adoption dates from work during the 1948-1951 interval: man's increase of power over nature, per capita and per square kilometer of the Earth's surface, may be described, in rough approximation, as follows.[8]

It is to be said, that that ordered increase of man's power over nature, per capita and per square-kilometer of the Earth's surface, is always expressed in the form of the outcome of successive, revolutionary, realized discoveries of physical principle. It is shown, on physical grounds, that experimentally validatable, revolutionary discoveries of physical principle, form orderable, if not linear, or otherwise simple sequences.[9] It is

the realization of those sequences, whose accumulation correlates with an increase of mankind's potential (physical) power over nature. During 1948-1951, as today, the argument remains, that this connection is typified by the treatment of an experimentally validated physical principle as the subsuming source of those applicable machine-tool designs, and analogous principles, which are to be recognized as "technologies."[10]

The second of the three principles, whose discovery also dates from the 1948-1951 interval, was the apprehension of the fact, that those same processes of creative mentation, by means of which experimentally validated, original (i.e., "revolutionary") discoveries of physical principle are generated, in response to deductively insoluble paradoxes of experimental physics, are processes identical in their nature to the validatable solution for the type of paradox rightly identified as *metaphor*, as such metaphors are unique to *strictly Classical* modes of musical, poetic, dramatic, and plastic composition in art. This second principle, which is contrary to the currently popular, erroneous notion of a division of art (e.g., *Geisteswissenschaft*) from physical science (e.g., *Naturwissenschaft*),[11] is the key point of reference for the present report.

The third of these principles, dating from 1952, was my recognition of a relevant implication of that generalized notion of a Keplerian, multiply-connected manifold, first defined as an amendment to the work of Carl Gauss, in Bernhard Riemann's 1854, revolutionary habilitation dissertation.[12] From a reexamination of Rie-

philosopher Martin Heidegger called "thrownness." Helga Zepp-LaRouche, in a Sept. 3, 1994 speech ("Ghost of Martin Heidegger Haunts Cairo Conference," **Executive Intelligence Review**, Sept. 12, 1994), described Heidegger's existentialism as follows: "'Man, in the course of the history of Occidental culture,' says Heidegger, 'has forgotten the essentials of human life. People live life in an unactual way, and they look for entertainment in their flight from death agony. The actuality of true life, lies in the banal, basic experience of the being-thrownness'— *Geworfenheit*, that is, you are thrown into history, and plop, there you are." Heidegger was a major influence on Jean-Paul Sartre.

8. Lyndon H. LaRouche, Jr., **So, You Wish to Learn All About Economics?**, second edition, (Washington, D.C.: EIR News Service, 1995).
9. Consider the intersecting, but distinct contributions to the founding of a science of electrodynamics by Ampère, Fresnel, Wilhelm Weber, Gauss, Riemann, et al. See Laurence Hecht, "The Significance of the 1845 Gauss-Weber Correspondence," **21st Century Science & Technology**, Fall 1996, and Laurence Hecht, "Optical Theory in the 19th Century, and the Truth about Michelson-Morley-Miller," **21st Century Science & Technology**, Spring 1998. To be emphasized, on this ac-

count, are Ampère-Weber on the "longitudinal force," and Fresnel-Riemann on refraction and retarded propagation.
10. Formally, the introduction of "machine-tool design" into modern economy, originates with the work of Lazare Carnot, especially his role in the economic-military mobilization of 1792-1794. However, the "machine-tool-design era" is dated to a later time, the 1861-1876 mobilization of the U.S. economy. The "industrial revolution" proper was thus launched from the United States, from whence direct U.S. influence spread it into Bismarck's Germany (1877), Meiji Restoration Japan, and the Russia of Alexander II.
11. I.e., the doctrine of G.W.F. Hegel's politically reactionary ally, the neo-Kantian Romantic Karl Friedrich Savigny: i.e., the absolute separation of *Geisteswissenschaft* from *Naturwissenschaft*. In a cruder version, this is also the doctrine of "art for art's sake:" that there is no rational principle underlying the determination of value in art, that art is the arbitrary taste of artists and their audiences.
12. Bernhard Riemann, *Über die Hypothesen, welcher der Geometrie zu Grunde liegen*, **Bernhard Riemanns Gesammelte Mathematische Werke**, H. Weber, ed. (New York: Dover Publications reprint, 1953). This Kepler-Gauss-Riemann standpoint, is identical with Leibniz's insistence that the "infinitesimals" of his calculus are not linear, but are intervals of non-constant curvature.

mann's habilitation dissertation at that time, I recognized, that his discovery provides the indispensable, meta-mathematical basis for comprehending, and integrating, the function of validated creative discoveries of principle, not only in physical science, but also Classical art-forms.[13] Furthermore, my appreciation of Riemann's discovery was novel, in the degree that it is associated with an explicitly Platonic notion of the relevant principles of ontology in general. I contended, that this metaphysical connection to the ontology of Platonic ideas, is strongly implied in Riemann's work by a comparison of several among his writings from that period;[14] in my own statement of the case then, as restated here for the case of music, the notion is explicit.

If one is to adhere to the principles of a Classical humanist education, one must account for the origin, and deeper, present-day implication of these three, interrelated discoveries. One must take into account that consuming occupation with modern philosophy which had dominated my adolescent years.[15] All of these discoveries of the 1948-1952 interval, were rooted in an adolescent choice of the world-view of Gottfried Leibniz. During adolescence, my adherence to Leibniz's standpoint,[16] included a specific, explicit opposition to the educational dogmas of John Dewey,[17] and coincided with my continuing rejection, to the present day, of the Seventeenth and Eighteenth Centuries' English and French reductionists generally.[18] It was during the later

phase of that adolescent study, that I first defined my opposition to that paradigmatic, neo-Aristotelean attack on Leibniz which is central to Immanuel Kant's famous *Critiques*.[19]

On account of those same principles of Classical humanist education, one must emphasize, that there was nothing accidental in the fact, that the combined, 1948-1952 discoveries themselves, were prompted chiefly by my impassioned concern to expose the essential, neo-Kantian fraud underlying certain radical-positivist innovations introduced by two prominent devotees of Bertrand Russell. Those latter, targeted frauds, were, the radically reductionist "information theory" (e.g., radically positivist "linguistics") of Professor Norbert Wiener,[20] and the closely related hoax, the "systems analysis" of Professor John von Neumann.[21]

Similarly, the tactic which I chose for development of my 1948-1952 refutations of, initially, Wiener and, later, von Neumann, was a conviction which I had adopted during the war-time 1940s, that the problems of a theory of knowledge posed by Kant's *Critiques*, must be attacked from the vantage-point of a general science of physical (as distinct from monetary-financial) economy—i.e., man's self-perpetuating increase of his species' practical power over nature. This must be a sci-

13. Bernhard Riemann, *Zur Psychologie und Metaphysik*, **Werke,** op. cit., pp. 509-520.

14. E.g., *Geistesmasse*, in Riemann's posthumously published manuscripts on the subject of metaphysics, **Werke**, op. cit.

15. In Classical culture, no principle is ever merely learned. A principle must be known, rather than merely learned. To know a principle, is both to experience in oneself the process which generates the discovery, and to experience the equivalent of a crucial-experimental proof of that principle. By "principle," one signifies a law of nature which can not be derived by deduction, but only by discovering an experimentally validatable idea which solves an otherwise insoluble contradiction in previously established knowledge.

16. Especially, at that time, the **Theodicy, Monadology,** and **Clarke-Leibniz Correspondence**.

17. A reading of works by and on the subject of Dewey's educational programs, during my fourteenth year, in the Ninth Grade, left me with a sense of being degraded by, and hostile to submission to the philosophy of education integral to the courses of instruction offered in secondary education at that time. It was this issue which led me to the subsequent years impassioned occupation with the issue of Kant's **Critique of Pure Reason**.

18. E.g., the reductionism of such followers of Paolo Sarpi as Francis Bacon, Galileo Galilei, Thomas Hobbes, René Decartes, John Locke,

Bernard Mandeville, David Hume, and such followers of Antonio Conti as Voltaire and the French "Encyclopaedists."

19. At that time, Kant's **Critique of Pure Reason** and **Prolegomena**. See also, on Leonhard Euler's resort to the fraud of *petitio principii* in his own effort to supply an argument against Leibniz's **Monadology**: Lyndon H. LaRouche, Jr., "Pope's Havana Homily Defends Nation-State," **Executive Intelligence Review**, February 6, 1998, p. 51.

20. E.g., Norbert Wiener, **Cybernetics** (New York: []John Wiley & Sons, 1948). The root of Wiener's "information theory," is to be found in the founding of Russell's school of linguistics in the relevant collaboration of Russell, Karl Korsch, Carnap, Hutchins, Harris, et al. Russell's 1938 "unification of science" project, is the setting for the MIT school of linguistics and "artificial intelligence" of Noam Chomsky and Marvin Minsky.

21. After John von Neumann's work had received a devastating blow at the hands of Kurt Gödel's 1930-1931 works "On Formally Undecidable Propositions of **Principia Mathematica** and Related Systems" and *Discussion on Providing a Foundation for Mathematics*, **Collected Works**, Vol. I, (New York: Oxford University Press, 1986), von Neumann shifted into the field of a mathematical theory of games. By 1938, von Neumann fell into the absurdity of claiming that he could reduce economics to a matter of solutions for simultaneous linear inequalities. In this connection, von Neumann fell into collaboration with Oskar Morgenstern, producing the radically absurd doctrine of their **Theory of Games & Economic Behavior**, third edition (Princeton: Princeton University Press, 1953). In a similar vein, von Neumann, like Wiener, proposed the possibility of defining "artificial intelligence" as an offspring of a linear digital computer-system.

ence whose elementary focus is the adducing of those principles which govern mankind's manifest, unique potential for willfully increasing our species' *potential relative population-density*. This ordering must be associated with the impact and correlatives of the generation of scientific, technological, and cultural progress.[22]

In service of the same, Classical humanist principles of accounting for one's own knowledge, today's continuing, central, practical issue of world culture and politics, which I shall bring into sharper focus here, is the fact, of the increasing political hegemony, within modern European world-culture, of an anti-Renaissance, reductionist, and specifically Venetian world-outlook. That perverted outlook, is, most notably, the legacy of Pietro Pomponazzi,[23] Paolo Sarpi,[24] Antonio Conti,[25] et al. This Venetian influence has established,

as its legacy, a specific pathological trait, a trait which has been imposed upon the most widely accepted beliefs and practice of modern European academic and related culture. The latter, sundry—variously Aristotelean, "neo-Aristotelean," "empiricist," "Cartesian," materialist, and "positivist"—trends in leading opinion, have established the hegemony of their common pathological dogma, the which implicitly demands a dichotomy between the idea of knowledge in general, such as the so-called "liberal arts," and the notion of rational behavior to be associated with physical science. This conflict is usefully compared with what British author C.P. Snow identified, more simplistically, as the "Two Cultures" dichotomy of modern European empiricist dogma.[26]

Despite presently hegemonic kinds of philosophically reductionist influences: since the influence of Classical Greek culture, especially the heritage of Plato and his Academy,[27] the best currents of European civilization had acquired a relatively clear, if not simple conception of an implicitly ordered relationship underlying the ordering of human social progress, the latter respecting both individual physical practice and demographic characteristics of cultures at those technological levels of practice. This is an ordering correlated, measurably, with notions of *relative potential population-density*. The notion of a correlation between an improvement in the demographic and related individual characteristics of populations, and the related role of applied scientific and technological progress in fostering advances in per-capita and per-square-kilometer power over nature, has supplied a clear practical standard for measuring what, until recently, had been recognized as "the idea of progress."[28]

However, although the idea of progress involved clear notions of ordering, and of related measurements, the inevitability of progress was not a matter of clearly established principle. It appeared, for example, that

22. The initial attack on this problem occurred, during the early 1940s, as a critique of Karl Marx's **Capital**. The writer's critical focus was on the devastating effects of Marx's refusal to consider the implications of "the technological compositions of capitals," a refusal, stated in Volume I, which supplies the crucial error in Marx's attempt, in his Volumes II and III, to construct an account of "simple" and "extended reproduction of capital." The technological issues which Marx evades, are the foundation for any scientific approach both to the understanding of the processes of physical economy generally, and to the origins of so-called "business cycles." On account of Marx's axiomatic error on this point, the four-volume edition of his **Capital** manuscripts, and related writings, absolutely does not meet the requirements of a science of extended social reproduction. Over the recent four decades, and longer, this has often been a persisting, crucial issue of attacks on the present writer by those esteeming themselves defenders of Marxist economics orthodoxy.

23. Pietro Pomponazzi (1462-1525). Padua's Pomponazzi emerged as a leading apologist for the opponents to the mid-Fifteenth-Century ecumenical Council of Florence. In his capacity, together with his student Cardinal Gasparo Contarini, as the leading opponent of the Fifteenth-Century Renaissance throughout Europe, he introduced the gnostic, Aristotelean dogma of Averroes et al. into the Venice-dominated, post-League of Cambrai, Sixteenth Century.

24. Paolo Sarpi (1552-1623). Sarpi, who was, from 1582 onward, the leader of the dominant faction of Venice, is notorious for his adoption of a radical version of Aristotelean formalism, a formalism derived from the model of William of Ockham. Sarpi was, in his time, the controller of the English monarchy of King James I, and the sponsor of such related notables as Francis Bacon, Galileo Galilei, and Thomas Hobbes. He is the founder of the British empiricist and Cartesian method.

25. Antonio Conti (1677-1749), famous as the creator of Voltaire and of the myth of Isaac Newton's calculus. He was the leading successor to the role of Paolo Sarpi in spreading the hegemony of the Eighteenth-Century versions of the British and French (anti-Renaissance) "Enlightenment" throughout Europe. Conti's influence, as expressed by Leonhard Euler, Lagrange, Laplace, and Augustin Cauchy, established the political hegemony of the radically reductionist faction in scientific teaching throughout European civilization, to the present day. The

notion of "linearity" in the infinitestimally small, and the related radical empiricism of the positivists Bertrand Russell, Norbert Wiener, John von Neumann, et al., are included among the products of this influence of Conti.

26. C.P. Snow, **Two Cultures and, the Scientific Revolution** (London and New York: Cambridge University Press, 1993 reprint).

27. "Plato and his Academy" embraces the work of Plato's followers, through the work of Archimedes' contemporary Eratosthenes.

28. The improvement of transportation, water management, and usable energy per capita and per square kilometer, are typical of those changes in basic economic infrastructure which have the same general effect as technological progress in general.

there exists no conceivable mathematical function of the ordinary type, the which would ensure that any valid advance in discovery of applicable physical principle should lead to the lawful generation of a next higher order of discovered principle of general practice. Indeed, even in the case of a valid discovery of principle, there was no clear assurance that society would accept an experimentally proven such principle as a rule for improved social practice. Taking as much as we know of the whole span of the human species' existence to date, human progress has been the likely, but uncertain outcome of history considered in the large.

To repeat the crucial point: It was clear to modern European civilization, that progress were always possible,[29] but that progress did not necessarily occur in the manner a simple notion of physical science suggested. Stagnation, or worse, demographic and physical retrogression, often occurred. In the long, combined history and pre-history of mankind, only a few strains of cultural development have not been cast aside, rightly, as failed cultures. In known history, the catastrophic persistence of oligarchical forms of society, such as those of the ancient Mesopotamians, the Romans, Byzantium, and the Aztecs, illustrate the frequent case, of cultures which, although more or less long-dominant, are best characterized as cultures ultimately self-doomed by their inherent lack of sufficient "moral fitness to survive."

We pivot our argument here upon the issues of that pathological, cultural-historical paradigm referenced by Friedrich Schiller.[30] We reference, so, the awful history of France's moral degeneration, during most of the periods following the outbreak of the French Revolution of 1789.[31] Excepting such great, exemplary achievements of 1792-1814, as were led by the circles of Lazare Carnot and Gaspard Monge's *Ecole Polytechnique*, the reconstructed France of Louis XI, which had continued until 1789 as the world's most developed nation-state, had, by 1789, turned sharply downward, away from the course implied by the Marquis de Lafayette's role in the American Revolution, into those "Enlightenment" orgies of moral degeneracy typified by followers of Robespierre, Barras, Napoleon Bonaparte, and the French positivists in general.

Schiller's intent in addressing this ominous, crucial failure of French culture, is elaborated in locations such as his *Über die Aesthetische Erziehung des Menschen*.[32] Nonetheless, although Schiller's intent ought to be clear from his own writings, the deeper, most crucial, *ontological* implications of his argument, as in the Fifth Letter of that series, appear to be grasped by most among his putative admirers only in a relatively superficial way, not grasped in the sense of a relevant, cognitively rigorous notion of ontology. It is those ontological implications which I am specially qualified to address, as I do here. Those ontological issues, and their practical implications for world politics today, are the essential subject of this report.

In a report to be published in a forthcoming issue, we focus upon the case of music, to illustrate the ontological basis for Schiller's insight into the role of cultural development. There, we focus upon the exemplary case of Classical musical, *motivic thorough-composition*, as located by W.A. Mozart in the foundations supplied by such works of J.S. Bach as **A Musical Offering**.[33] That development, from

29. Admittedly, influential radical empiricists, such as Bertrand Russell and his followers, did not share that optimistic view.

30. Friedrich Schiller references the failure of the French people to seize the opportunity of the French Revolution in two locations. In the Fifth Letter on the Aesthetical Education of Man, he writes that "a *physical* possibility seems given, to place the law upon the throne, to honor man finally as an end in himself and to make true freedom the basis of political union. Vain hope! The *moral* possibility is wanting; and the generous moment finds an unresponsive people." **Friedrich Schiller, Poet of Freedom**, Vol. I (New York: Schiller Institute, 1985) p. 230. He also wrote the following epigram entitled "The Moment":
"A momentous epoch hath the cent'ry engender'd,
Yet the moment so great findeth a people so small."
Ibid., p. 325.

31. Not only under the Jacobins and the Napoleonic regimes, but also the post-1898 Third Republic, the Fourth Republic, and the Mitterrand regimes.

32. F. Schiller, *Über die Ästhetische Erziehung des Menschen in einer Reihe von Briefen*, in **Friedrich Schiller Sämtliche Werke: Fünfter Band**, Gerhard Fricke and Herbert G. Goepfert, eds. (München: Carl Hanser Verlag, 1993). An English translation is in **Friedrich Schiller: Poet of Freedom**, Vol. I, op. cit.

33. Briefly, J.S. Bach's development of a form of polyphony situated with respect to the Florentine *bel canto* voice-training standard, led into a determination of both pitch and of counterpoint derived from a rigorous application of the principles of a multiply-connected manifold. The related treatment of the principle of polyphonic (e.g., "cross voice") inversions led into such crucial Bach works as his **A Musical Offering** and **The Art of the Fugue**. The rigorous study of this aspect of J.S. Bach's methods of composition, from the standpoint of **A Musical Offering**, steered Wolfgang Mozart directly (e.g., the K.475 **Fantasy**) into that method of *motivic thorough-composition* which is the characteristic of the post-1783 work of Mozart, Haydn, Beethoven, et al. It is this process of development, from J.S. Bach through Brahms, which defines the Classical, as opposed to Romantic, et al. notions of musical composition.

Bach, through Haydn,[34] Mozart, Beethoven, and Brahms, is employed here as a model of the ontological function at the core of Schiller's principle of aesthetical education. We include, as crucial, reference to Goethe's poor judgment on Mozart's and Beethoven's song settings for Goethe's poems, and the related case of Franz Schubert's sharing Schiller's opposition to Goethe on this matter of practice.[35]

What we offer, thus, is not a complete treatment of the role of Classical culture. Our task here, is to lead the reader into a breakthrough in recognizing, from the example of music, the nature of the *ontological* principle involved in Classical culture, as a whole.

## 2. Art as Science

In the history of ideas of principle as represented by the work of Plato, the relatively brief **Parmenides** dialogue occupies a special place of relevance. From the standpoint of that **Parmenides** and related writings, Plato's notion of what he defines as *ideas* is presented by him as a defense of the seminal contributions of the school of Pythagoras, against the anti-Pythagoras, Eleatic faction of reductionism. These Eleatics are epitomized by the dialogue's Parmenides. Constantly, the echoes of Heraclitus' ontological standpoint, "nothing is constant but change," reverberate in the crucial passages of Plato's dialogue.

The central issue attacked in that dialogue, is the same ontological blunder which underlies all of the reductionist tradition, from the Eleatics, through the sophists and Aristotle, through to the modern empiricists, materialists, and positivists. Given a sequence of developments which corresponds to some ordered change of principle, how might we conceptualize a higher principle which underlies and generates the ordered sequence of relevant, successful changes in apparent principle?

In art generally, as in Plato's dialogues, the dominant role performed by the composition, is the quality of *ontological surprise*, a point in the development at which a paradoxical transformation occurs in the import of that composition, a point at which the composer leads the audience away from a narrow focus upon the apparent, relatively literal, merely formal expression of the ongoing subject-matter, into what proves to be an ordered series of successive, more or less kaleidoscopic transformations in meaning, in principle. That principle which subsumes such an ordering of successive, mutually contradictory principles, appears, thus, ontologically, as the true, subsuming subject-matter of the artistic composition.

That true subject is the location of the *ontological* quality of the composition, the location of the *ontological* quality of all Classical art.

For example, in Shakespeare's **Hamlet**, especially the notable Third Act soliloquy, Hamlet is confronted by the choice of either clinging to his "macho's" habitual, petty, paranoid, swashbuckling world-outlook, which assures his self-imposed doom, or venturing into a new quality of world-outlook, the latter which he rejects as a "bourn from which no traveller" has returned. There is virtually no difference between that Hamlet and those tragic statesmen, today, faced with the inevitable collapse and disintegration of the world's present financial and monetary system, who prefer to work within the bounds of adapting, as "practical politicians," to the doomed system, rather than risk the escape to safety from the doomed system, by adopting what they presently abhor as a radically new form: a bourn from which no traveller has returned. For them, it is more comfortable to return to the old, familiar, diseased slut, than to couple with a healthy immigrant.

On this account, no great playwright ever composed fiction. Just as Aeschylos' **Prometheus Bound** is nothing but a truthful presentation of the paradoxical principle then governing the real universe of ancient Greek culture, so neither Shakespeare nor Schiller ever composed mere fiction, mere existentialists' entertainment. The essence of Classical tragedy and poetry is the equivalence of truth and beauty. No great tragedian ever composed a drama in which the principle of history exhibited on stage was not a truthful representation of a relevant principle of real-life history, a principle

---

34. The evidence is, that Professor Norbert Brainin is probably unique among contemporaries in his recognition of Haydn's initial demonstration of principles of thorough-composition, although the discovery of the more general such principle is dated to the work of Wolfgang Mozart, beginning 1782-1783. Nonetheless, without Haydn's work in carrying the development of composition beyond the standard established by C.P.E. Bach, Mozart would have lacked the foundation upon which to grasp the fuller implications of J.S. Bach's **A Musical Offering**, implications upon which a general principle of motivic thorough-composition depended.

35. Chapter 11, "Artistic Beauty: Schiller versus Goethe," **A Manual on the Rudiments of Tuning and Registration**, Book I, (Washington, D.C.: Schiller Institute, 1992).

expressed in a real-life-based apprehension of historical specificity.

Contrast Classical tragedy with the degeneracy which has taken over the modern staging of even Classical opera and dramas. The Classical stage has been replaced by the theater of cheap tricks performed by aid of irrelevant sensual effects and paranoid symbolisms. Take, for example, the late Orson Welles' famous 1937-1938 Mercury Theater, "relevant" staging of Shakespeare, as a notable example of this presently continuing degeneracy of practice.[36]

In the Classical theater, from Aeschylos through Shakespeare and Schiller, the medium deployed on stage is what appears, at first, to be nothing but a literal representation of what the dramatist intended to portray: without symbolism, without cheap sensual, or other "special effects." The substance of the drama emerges as an eerie something which is occurring behind the scene, within what the author and audience apprehend as the minds of the characters. This is a different, higher dimension than the literal actions on stage, a dimension of paradox and metaphor. In a valid performance, the mind of the audience is shifted from the literal drama as such, to the eerie sense of some principle of the mind which intervenes to change the character of the literal events on stage. The drama is thus shifted from the literal drama on stage, to the drama within the mind of the audience.

Thus, it was Schiller's principle, that the audience must emerge from the theater better people than they had entered that theater. In great Classical tragedy, the audience is horrified at the discovery that it entered the theater with a disposition for condoning the kinds of errors which led the tragic figures on stage to the latters' doom. It is in that eerie sense of irony, that the true drama lies; there, thus, within the audience itself, lies the true *ontological* dimension of the Classical drama.

Consider the case of Schiller's **Don Carlos**. Apart from the sole hero(ine) of the tragedy, Elizabeth, Don Carlos, Posa, and King Philip II, are each gripped, like Shakespeare's Hamlet, by a compelling devotion to some fatal degree of relative spiritual littleness in themselves. World-historical roles are more or less evaded, out of small-minded attachment to small-minded family and kindred personal considerations. Among the three principal male characters, the otherwise flawed Posa, alone, rises to the relatively highest level; he recognizes, if without the necessary consistency, that the alternative to the doom of Spain's monstrous follies in the Netherlands, is to rise to the level of world-historical statesmen: Not what might seem to offer personal success, but to make one's living a meaningful role in shaping history for the betterment of future mankind.[37]

There is no fiction, no petty moralizing, in the writing of Schiller's **Don Carlos**; it is a *truthful* account of those principles underlying the historical specificity of that senseless butchery in which the contending forces of the Netherlands' warfare went down to mutual bestiality, the folly by which Spain doomed itself to degenerating from a world power into a morbid relic of its earlier pretenses to grandeur. The audience, gripped by such great tragic compositions, is induced to sense the paradox, the irony, the metaphor lodged in the discrepancy between the character's personal motivations and that same character's world-historical accountability for the outcome of current events. In Schiller's composition of the drama, the truth lies not in the selection of literal events on stage; the truth lies in the artful juxtaposition of those conflicts of principle—those meta-

36. Welles's **Caesar**, adapted from Shakespeare, opened on Nov. 11, 1937 at the Mercury Theater in New York. The staging and costumes were done to suggest the fascist regimes of Hitler and Mussolini, with what was described as "Nuremberg lighting." See Orson Welles and Peter Bogdanovich, **This is Orson Welles** (New York: HarperCollins, 1992).

37. See F. Schiller on the role of Elizabeth, as contrasted with that of Posa, in **Don Carlos**. Posa, finding the King in a state of mind that disposed him, in his loneliness, to seek an adviser other than his usual court lackeys, seizes the moment of opportunity to passionately reveal, to the most powerful ruler in the world, Posa's own innermost thoughts, along with his perspective for securing happiness for the people of Flanders. That he does so, is understandable; but the fact that he allows himself to believe for longer than an instant, that in Philip he had found his instrument for effecting the "greatest possible realization of individual freedom, alongside the greatest flourishing of the state," borders on delusion.

Worse still, is the fact that for this and other reasons, he breaks his alliance with Don Carlos, without informing the latter of the changed situation ("Why show a sleeping person the storm cloud that is hanging over his head?"), and that he even resorts to court intrigues, ostensibly in order to save Carlos. And finally, when his plan fails, he sacrifices himself out of egotistical motives: "...and thus, on the contrary, it is entirely in keeping with the character of this heroic enthusiast, that in order to shorten this route [out of a condition of despondency], he seeks to place himself once again in high esteem by means of some extraordinary act, by means of a momentary heightening of his being," Schiller writes in his "Letters on Don Carlos." Cf. F. Schiller, *Briefe über Don Carlos*, **Friedrich Schiller: Sämtliche Werke** (München: Carl Hauser Verlag, 1981), Vol. II, *Dramen II*, Letters Six through Twelve, pp. 244-267.

phors—which account for the tragic, actual history of referenced, real-life events.

Indeed, it should be noted that, for reasons we shall identify below, all great tragedy is grounded in historical specificity.[38] If Rome of the doomed Julius Caesar is the subject chosen, then it is the historically specific crisis of the process of continued degeneration of the Republic of Rome which is the matter addressed by Shakespeare. Similarly, the real, self-imposed doom of Spain is the historically specific location of the subject of Schiller's **Don Carlos**, just as Aeschylos' **Prometheus Bound** is historically specific to the self-induced doom of the ancient oligarchical Greece dominated by the pervasive influence of the satanic cult of Apollo.

In drama, as in Classical poetry, the essential difference between mere fiction and true art, is that the artistic content of great tragic compositions lies not within the literal events arranged on stage; the content lies in the successively emerging conflicts of principle, that succession of surprising ideas which prompts the audience to leave the theater better people than they entered it, shortly before.

In music, the same principle of Classical artistic composition appears in a different form of expression. Nonetheless, the same ontological principle, as implicit in the paradoxes of Plato's **Parmenides**, is the governing principle underlying those transformations in physical science which are the outgrowth of successive, validated discoveries of physical principle. In fact, it is this same principle, as expressed in the form of Classical artistic composition, which is the governing moral principle of realized scientific progress.

To this purpose, shift our focus from the Classical tragedy of Aeschylos, Shakespeare, or Schiller, to the manner in which the same principle of artistic composition is developed, with relative perfection, in the progress of post-Renaissance musical composition from J.S. Bach through Haydn, Mozart, Beethoven, Schubert, Chopin, Schumann, and Brahms.[39] To that end, let us now define the historical setting in which the importance of modern Classical musical composition is situated. We emphasize the development of modern Euro-pean culture which was built upon the foundations of the Fifteenth-Century "Golden Renaissance," contrasting this to the presently dominant role of the anti-Renaissance, Aristotelean and Ockhamite "Enlightenment," which gained increasing hegemony in post-League of Cambrai, Sixteenth-Century Europe.

To restate the nature of the connections: the essence of the matter, is the precise agreement between the principles of physical-scientific discovery, as these principles might be adduced from the accomplishments of Bernhard Riemann, with the principles of such Classical art as Eighteenth- and Nineteenth-Century Classical, musical motivic thorough-composition. For the purpose of locating those developments of Renaissance science leading into the emergence of Classical motivic thorough-composition, Cardinal Nicolaus of Cusa[40] is the founder of modern experimental physical science, a role which emerged from his **De Docta Ignorantia**[41] and those other, later writings,[42] which educated, and otherwise inspired such founders of modern science as Luca Pacioli, Leonardo da Vinci, William Gilbert, and Johannes Kepler.[43]

In method, Cusa, is, in turn, a follower of the great Plato; his work is in the same Platonic tradition so clearly adopted for theology by the Apostles Paul and

---

38. For a more fulsome treatment of this principle of historical specificity, see the treatment of the case of world-historical individual, below.

39. Contrast the success of the first movement of Frederic Chopin's echoes of Beethoven's Opus 111, with the pathetic folly of Franz Liszt's notoriously failed effort to replicate the same Mozart-Beethoven legacy of the K. 475 **Fantasy**.

40. Nicolaus of Cusa (1401-1464). See Helga Zepp-LaRouche, "Nicolaus of Cusa and the Council of Florence" **Fidelio**, Spring 1992, pp. 17-22.

41. **De Docta Ignorantia (On Learned Ignorance)**, trans. by Jasper Hopkins as **Nicholas of Cusa on Learned Ignorance** (Minneapolis: Arthur M. Banning Press, 1985).

42. The principal writings on the subject of scientific topics by Cardinal Nicolaus of Cusa, composed after **De Docta Ignorantia**, include: "On Conjectures," "On Beryllus," "On the Game of Spheres," "The Vision of God," "On Mathematical Complements," "On Geometrical Transformation," "Quadrature of the Circle," "The Golden Proposition in Mathematics," and "The Layman on Experiments Done with Weight-Scales."

43. For the case of Luca Pacioli and his collaborator, Leonardo da Vinci, see Pacioli, **De Divina Proportione** (1497) (Vienna: 1896; Milano: Silvana Editoriale, 1982, facsimile of 1497), Chapter 1.

For Kepler on the "divine" Cusa, see Johannes Kepler, **Mysterium Cosmographicum (The Secret of the Universe)**, trans. by A.M. Duncan (New York: Abaris Books, 1981), p. 93: "For in one respect Nicholas of Cusa and others seem to me divine, that they attached so much importance to the relationship between a straight line and a curved line and dared to liken a curve to God, a straight line to his creatures...." Kepler frequently acknowledged his debt to William Gilbert, for the application of the primacy of the field (structure of space) to magnetic and, by analogy, solar gravitational phenomena, over the materialism of Paolo Sarpi and Sarpi's agents Francis Bacon and Galileo. Gilbert was attacked by Bacon in multiple printed locations: Bacon's "New Organon," "On Principles and Origins," "On the Ebb and Flow of the Sea," for his experimental method rooted in hypothesis.

John.[44] The special emphasis to be supplied here, is, that although the glimmerings of the notion of Classical *ideas* do antedate Plato's dialogues, it is with Plato that the nature and role of the *idea* first appears in a rigorous and clearly replicatable form. This principle of the *idea*, which underlies the work of such Fifteenth-Century *Golden Renaissance* figures as Cusa, is key to grasping the ontological implications of Friedrich Schiller's arguments in his **Aesthetische Erziehung** and related writings.[45] Here, by way of that Platonic *Golden Renaissance*, art found its essential unity with science.

In narrowest focus, the *idea* which distinguishes the essence of Classical musical composition, from Romantic and other alternatives, exemplifies the kind of Platonic *idea* we must associate with Schiller's attention to . . . *Der Gegenstand des sinnlichen Triebes*[46] (the object of the sensual impulse). It is for that reason, that we have selected the case of Classical music to illustrate the principle of culture in general. For this reason, it may be said, that the general principle of all Classical art, is most simply illustrated by the case for the principles of Classical motivic thorough-composition in music.

The ontological issues are sharply defined. It is not the notes—the tones, chords, overtones, etc., as such—which form the self-evident, sensuous elements of Classical musical composition. The substance of Classical music, in its defining, subsuming process of development, from Bach through Brahms, lies within the same creative-mental process of development which governs the ordering of metaphor expressed as the coherent unfolding of a work of Classical motivic thorough-composition.[47] It is in that ordering, not any collection, or interpretation of the individual tones as such, that the ontological actuality of Classical musical composition and performance lies.

Agreed: in Classical composition, the composer's intent must be followed scrupulously. Echoes of the decadent, symbolism-ridden, anti-Renaissance mannerism of reactionary, mid-Sixteenth-Century European art, are not to be tolerated kindly. However, the function of that rigorous respect for the composer's intent, is not rightly intended to represent a strict school-book interpretation of the score, as if according to the vanity of some poor pedant's conceits. The strict observance of the composer's intent, is to ensure that the paradoxes (e.g., metaphors) generated within the composition, are clearly defined ambiguities, paradoxes (metaphors) whose resolution must be the idea corresponding to the artistic intent of that choice of motivic thorough-composition taken in its wholeness.

Contrary to today's widely taught musicological dogmas, the "substance" of Classical music is located outside any linear measure, outside any domain of constant curvature; what we hear, and what should be performed, thus, must be heard "between the notes," not within them. It is not the notes we must hear; it is not merely a matter of the "right tuning" of the well-tempered scale. So, for J.S. Bach, as for Mozart et al., after him, we must never hear intervals merely within voice-parts, or even merely across voices, except that we *also* hear the totality of the implied, complementary inversions within and across the voices, as these unfold in the course of that motivic development which is the unity of the composition as an indivisible whole.[48]

As we shall show in the forthcoming report, it is the ordering of that "in-betweenness," which is the rudimentary location of that musical developmental process, the which is heard primarily with the mind, and only in a lesser degree the ear as such. Monkeys with perfect pitch do not make music. From J.S. Bach on, well-tempered tuning, whether within the individual composition, or subsuming the succession of development of musical ideas by great Classical composers, is a reflection of a coherent process of thoroughly composed motivic development; it is in the process of com-

44. For example, the treatment of *agapē* in Paul's **I Corinthians** 13.
45. "Letters on the Aesthetical Education of Man," **Friedrich Schiller, Poet of Freedom**, Vol. I, op. cit., pp. 223-98; "On Grace and Dignity," "Kallias or, On the Beautiful," **Friedrich Schiller, Poet of Freedom**, Vol. II (Schiller Institute: Washington, D.C., 1988), pp. 337-395, 482-526; "Philosophical Letters," "On the Pathetic" and "On the Sublime," **Friedrich Schiller, Poet of Freedom**, Vol. III (Schiller Institute: Washington, D.C., 1990), pp. 197-225, 227-271.
46. Friedrich Schiller, **Über die Ästhetische Erziehung des Menschen in Einer Reihe von Briefen**, op. cit., *Fünfzehnter Brief*, p. 614.
47. For an example of this, see Mindy Pechenuk on the function of the Lydian principle in Mozart's thorough composition of his **Ave Verum Corpus** motet. Mindy Pechenuk, "Mozart's Ave Verum Corpus," **Fidelio**, Winter 1996, pp. 34-45.

48. Among the very best demonstrations of that principle of performance is a Wilhelm Furtwängler recording of Franz Schubert's great C-Major Symphony (available on Music & Arts label, MUA 826). Other leading conductors' performances have a tendency toward a "pasted together" quality, by contrast with the gripping unity of motivic thorough-composition which Furtwängler achieves, and sustains, from the initial attack, onward.

position, that the required coherence of the performance must lie.[49] No mere computer could ever compose, or perform—or hear—such music.

On account of such underlying principles, Cusa's role as the initiator of modern experimental science, situates him, historically, within the "Golden Renaissance," as the most relevant, Platonic point of reference, for uncovering the essential unity of modern science and the accompanying development of Classical culture, Classical musical culture included.

## A Matter of Passion

Using the case for Classical musical composition as paradigmatic, three propositions are to be addressed.

• First, how do we demonstrate a common ordering for both Classical artistic ideas—in Plato's sense of *idea*—and the ideas associated with experimentally validated, revolutionary discoveries of physical principle?

• Second, how do such ideas regulate both the impetus for such scientific progress, and the adoption of a corresponding, revolutionary practice?

• Third, how do Classical artistic ideas govern the moral motivation of a population, to the effect that the lack of such motivation usually results, erosively, or catastrophically, in a great cultural calamity such as that ongoing today?

The answer to those three questions is embedded, pervasively, in Plato's notion of *agapē,* as a motivation—a *passion*—which compels one to subordinate everything to concern for realizing justice and truth. This is the same passion, *agapē*, so prominently emphasized in the Apostle Paul's **I Corinthians** 13. The related issue, is the central feature of Plato's dialogues, that truth lies, ultimately, not in any fixed belief, but only in those valid, progressive changes in belief and behavior, the which supersede the paradoxes inhering in a previously established learning, with a validated discovery of higher principle.

Thus, the central feature of the thesis which we present here, is summarily the following.

Justice, truthfulness, and those creative powers by means of which we may discover valid, revolutionary principles of our universe, form a seamless whole, in which Classical culture, morality, and physical science, are united by a common passion for universal justice and truth.

These issues of truth and justice are associated empirically with tests of humanity's increased power over the physical universe, per capita, and per square kilometer of the Earth's surface. The increased development of the average newborn individual, the increase of per-capita power, the maintenance of the increase of those improvements in demographic and productive characteristics, and so forth, are typical of the evidence by means of which we may know that changes in knowledge for practice are in accord with the Creator's intent for the laws of the universe. This accords with justice, as *justice means a more adequate participation of each individual life as a world-historical being, a life so dwelling in the simultaneity of eternity, a mental life thus situated in the further development of the condition of all mankind.*

That passion for truth and justice, is rightly, and most conveniently identified as the *agapē* of both Plato and the Christian **New Testament**; it was, indeed, this Christian, Apostolic standpoint, based in *agapē*, which is the key to what emerged, during the period of the Fifteenth-Century *Golden Renaissance*, as modern European Classical culture. This passion, expressed as the powers of concentration through which valid discoveries of principle are prompted by metaphors, is the purest expression of reason, its *active* expression.

For example: contrast *reason* and mere *logic*, as opponents of one another. Where is the *passion* in a formal, deductive logic? The question itself is a contradiction in terms! Without the passion of relentlessly extended concentration, how might we discover the principle which overcomes a defiant paradox? Without the passion for truth, how would we be impelled to refuse to accept less than the recognition, or new discovery of such a principle?

The notion of a "dispassionate" search for truth, is a contradiction in terms. Logic as such, is morally dead, or, better said, outrightly immoral because it is amoral.

---

49. Start with Wolfgang Mozart's work of the 1782-1783 period. Locate a significant number of those compositions which Mozart derived from the same solution for Bach's **A Musical Offering** which is typified by the K.475 **Fantasy**. Next, arrange a set of compositions by Mozart, Beethoven, Schubert, Brahms, et al., which are derived from this same root. The K.475 "Lydian" modality, represents not only a principle of motivic thorough-composition for individual works; the development of successive works, by various such composers, expresses a higher principle of motivic thorough-composition than any single work of that species.

It is the creative impulses governed by an overriding passion for truth, that same passion, *agapē*, which separates the Christian from the moralizing hypocrite in **I Corinthians** 13, which are the only efficient source of truthfulness and justice. This is the passion which produces truth in the progress of physical science. This is the passion for truthfulness, the which is the essential distinction between Classical and allegedly "alternative" forms of art such as "the popular," Romantic, Modernist, Existentialist, Post-Modernist, etc.

This, as we shall see, leads us directly to the issue: If reason must be controlled by passions, rather than the dead hand of mere logic, what shall govern these passions? How shall we define the injunction of **I Corinthians** 13 on this account? By what means are such passions uniquely efficient in guiding us to practices of truth and justice? How do we, then, distinguish, those passions and forms of passion which are irrational, from those contrary forms which are the seat and substance of reason? This is the issue of culture. This is the issue which places Classical culture morally and otherwise apart from and above all currently popular misconceptions of culture.

The role of passion in the composition and performance of Classical music, is to be located so. As we shall indicate by aid of the forthcoming report, summarizing Classical musical tuning, the medium of Classical motivic thorough-composition, as we have located that here, is the sensuous domain within which musical ideas are expressed as musical ideas.

To that effect, turn now to those aspects of Plato's dialectical method which bear more emphatically on the matters of physical science.

## 3. The Principle of Hypothesis

The formalist, such as that pathetic creature, the mere logician, is a reductionist duped into believing that definitions, axioms, and postulates are given implicitly beforehand (as if *a priori*). The formalist presupposes, that one might discover such definitions, axioms, and postulates by means of deduction, a method of deduction which presumes to recognize these terms as if they had been given *a priori*. On the basis of such presumptions, such as those presumed by an Aristotle or Immanuel Kant, it is decreed that all acceptable theorems are derived by deduction from those initial presumptions.

The Socratic method of Plato proceeds in a directly opposite direction.

With Plato, one begins with propositions being entertained as prospective theorems, and then follows the approach taken in his dialogues, as a way of searching out discoverable fallacies in those underlying presumptions (definitions, axioms, and postulates) which are the adducible motives for those propositions which our prejudices have imposed upon us. The challenging of such prejudices, provides the user of Plato's method with what appears to be, for the moment, a refined array of mutually non-contradictory definitions, axioms, and postulates; this refined array, taken as a whole, is an *hypothesis*. For example, what was traditionally taught to modern students as Euclidean geometry was such an hypothesis.

The method of Plato starts with the recognition that all propositions, and, therefore, all hypotheses, including what were previously the most refined ones, must include some significant, axiomatic fallacy of some kind. In the method of Plato, we show that a sufficiently rigorous such exploration of previously accepted sets of definitions, axioms, and postulates, leads us to what are empirically contrary, mutually contradictory results. If that discovered contradiction is itself empirically truthful up to that point, then there must exist some previously overlooked, or unknown principle— some new definition, axiom, or postulate—which, as correction, resolves that contradiction. The result of a validated such correction represents a radically new set of definitions, axioms, and postulates: in other words, a new hypothesis.

Truth, then, does not lie in any one choice of hypothesis. Such deductively consistent hypotheses are merely conditional upon such tests; there is no certainty of settled truth in any method of deduction. Truth lies in the always radically revolutionary process, by means of which valid new principles are generated, new principles which take into account the contradictions inhering in the previously proposed hypothesis. The method by which such new principles are ordered, in overcoming successively ordered contradictions, thus represents a notion of *higher hypothesis*, the latter a verifiable ordering principle which is demonstrated, repeatedly, to generate successively improved hypotheses. That notion of higher hypothesis coincides with the domain of *reason*, a domain above and beyond any mere logic, the domain within which truth and true knowledge lie.

Riemann's 1854 habilitation dissertation supplies us the exemplary case.

Given any physical hypothesis, eliminate all *a priori* notions of space, time, and other dimensionalities. In place of dimensions, employ principles which are each based on a crucial-experimental validation. These *n* principles, then constitute an *n-fold* manifold of physical principles: principles of physical space-time.

Next, given the case, in which experimental evidence shows a persistent error of magnitude in what had been earlier assumed to be a valid n-fold manifold.[50] Take the case, that there be no experimental error internal to the n-fold manifold as defined previously. In the case that the self-contradictory evidence is crucially valid, there must be some previously overlooked, hidden physical principle, which accounts for the fact that an otherwise empirically validated n-fold manifold is contradicted by some adducibly persistent, crucial margin of error. The task posed is twofold: first, to discover a principle which resolves this contradiction, and, second, to provide a crucial-experimental demonstration of both the validity of the new principle and the factor which must be measured as the margin of difference between the characteristic of the n-fold and its replacement, the (n+1)-fold manifold which supersedes it.

The lesson of Plato's **Parmenides** haunts us once more. In such a physical geometry, neither space by iself, nor time by itself, have an *a priori*, self-evident existence. Space exists only as an empirically defined physical principle; the same is the case for time. All other notions of dimensionality are subject to the same condition.

Such is Plato's dialectical method. Instead of fashioning an hypothesis from sheer prejudice, or other presumptions, use the Socratic method of dialectical negation, to locate errors of presumption, and to adduce principles which not only account for the falsity of earlier presumptions, but which are demonstrably a guide to the needed corrections.

The exemplary case is Cusa's discovery of a rigorous, superbly elementary proof, that, by the standard of Eratosthenes' "sieve," π is what mathematician Georg Cantor later defined as a transcendental magnitude, rather than merely a Classical-Greek, irrational magni-

tude, as Eratosthenes' contemporary and correspondent, Archimedes, had imagined it to be.[51]

To indicate the connection between Plato's dialectical method and Riemannian manifolds, compare the earliest known, reasonably valid forms of ancient sidereal-solar astronomical calendars.[52] From this,

---

50. Treat Wilhelm Weber's correction and proof of Ampère's notion of a *longitudinal*, or *angular* force as an example of this. See Laurence Hecht, "The Significance of the 1845 Gauss-Weber Correspondence," **21st Century Science & Technology,** Fall 1996.

51. See Lyndon H. LaRouche, Jr., "On The Subject of Metaphor," **Fidelio** Fall 1992. See also **Nicolaus of Cusa on Learned Ignorance**, trans. by Jasper Hopkins, pp. 52-53, and "On the Quadrature of the Circle," trans. by William F. Wertz, Jr. **Toward a New Council of Florence** (Washington, D.C.: Schiller Institute, 1995), pp. 595-610. Compare Archimedes, "Measurement of a Circle," and "Quadrature of the Parabola," in **The Works of Archimedes**, T.L. Heath, ed. (New York: Dover Publications), pp. 91-98 and 233-252. See also Lyndon H. LaRouche, Jr., "The Ontological Superiority of Nicolaus of Cusa's Solution Over Archimedes' Notion of Quadrature," **Fidelio**, Summer 1994, pp. 31-34.

Contrast the popularized, academic delusion, which, like Professor Felix Klein, insists that the proof of the transcendental quality of π was first established by the successive work of Hermite and Lindemann. Note, that Klein himself traces the hereditary origins of Hermite's and Lindemann's argument to what was in fact an outright, *petitio principii* hoax by Berlin-based avowed enemy of Gottfried Leibniz, Venetian asset Leonhard Euler. Euler's argument against Leibniz's monadology rests upon Euler's arbitrary adoption of an axiom which presumes perfect continuity of linear extension, down to the smallest infinitesimal. Euler's proof, and the derived arguments of Hermite, Lindemann, and Klein, is thus a product of Euler's assertion, as an axiom of his argument, of the very conclusion, against Leibniz, which he professes to have proven.

52. As a result of the ideological fanaticism of the British Israelite movement, the growth of political influence of Venice's clone, the Anglo-Dutch financier-maritime oligarchy, wild-eyed hoaxsters such as the London-based Victorian archeologists degraded archeology in general virtually to a search for the exact street address of Abraham in ancient Ur. As a result of this British cult's influence, the most generally accepted doctrines respecting history, physical science, and culture generally were pivotted upon the notorious Bishop Usher's dating of Creation to an event located in Mesopotamia circa 4004 B.C. One consequence of this British Israelite hoax, is the popular delusion which dates astronomy from the lunar obsessions of early Mesopotamia. Similarly, although it is readily demonstrated that the earlier civilization in Mespotamia was the Dravidian colony known as Sumer, the British Israelites insist that Sumer was founded by Semites. The latter dogma continues to be asserted by both fanatics and their dupes, a teaching deployed in the interest of dating Creation from the place where God's foot stood in 4004 B.C. In fact, known solar-sidereal calendars are dated to no later than Vedic calendars from between 6000 and 4000 B.C.; evidence of still more ancient solar-sidereal calendars is known. The related fact is, as the Greek Herotodus reported, that the ancient cultures of Sumer, Sheba (modern Yemen), Ethiopia, and Canaan, were colonies of an ancient Dravidian culture which dominated the maritime regions of South and Southeast Asia, probably long before the close of the last Ice Age. The modern cultural heritage of India and Southeast Asia, as in the case of Thailand, for example, is predominantly a result of interactions among Dravidian, Vedic, and Chinese cultural interactions over millennia.

derive a relatively simple type of multiply-connected manifold.

The simplest quality of change defined in respect to solar-sidereal observation, from a position on the surface of the Earth, is the solar day: apparently a circular orbit. The next choice, for example, could be the solar year. The next choice, might be the complexity of the apparent movement of Moon and Sun. A next one, the equinoctial cycle. A next one, is the evolutionary change of the solar orbit, a phenomenon associated with the periodicity of ice ages. And, so on. Kepler's adducing of the elliptical orbits from observation of Mars, is an example of this same approach.[53]

The universe, as far as we know it, is a wonderful, vastly, perhaps endlessly complex process. This complexity begins to be transparent as we attempt to define a relatively universal frame of reference, a reference with which to compare the depicting of some motion observed from a fixed point on Earth to the same motion represented by a more universal standpoint. As we increase the number of interacting orbits considered, and include sundry other kinds of regular, semi-regular, and other pulsations, we recognize that there could be no point in the universe so smally infinitesimal, that any interval of action could be linear. The universe is, thus, Leibniz's domain of a calculus of non-constant curvature.

That considered, we shift our focus from orbits and analogous periodicities and quasi-periodicities, to physical principles. We view the universe as a multiply-connected manifold of such physical principles. This is Bernhard Riemann's domain, in which we are supplied no estimate of foreseeable limits to the number of such colligating principles. We abandon the notions of "dimensions" in their naive sense, in favor of an orderable accumulation of successive physical principles.

Looking at this matter from Riemann's standpoint, we have a useful way of defining a transfinite architecture for scientific progress. For this purpose, scientific progress, as envisaged by Nicolaus of Cusa,[54] is expressed in chiefly two ways.

In the first approximation, the experimental physical science of Cusa obliges us to recognize and prove outright fallacies, such as the fallacy of Archimedes' argument on the squaring of the circle, in previously enshrined scientific opinion.[55] In the next approximation, we are presented with more interesting challenges. In the leading features of the internal history of modern scientific progress since Cusa, we have to consider something other than pure and simple fallacies. In the best scientific work of discovery, we have to consider the cases, in which a particular colligating set of principles is in error only because it lacks some additional principle. On this account, at some point in the history of scientific progress, physics, for example, exhibits to us some newly discovered, persistent margin of empirical error, which we must suspect to correspond to existence of some previously unrecognized, additional physical principle. Thus, physical science assumes the form of a process of transformation from a valid n-fold manifold of physical principle, to a higher one of (n+1)-fold manifold.

In the latter type of case, we are presented with the case in which some physics, for example, was truthfully constructed, yet is shown, now, to be also untrue. This is a paradox of the type appropriately recognized as a metaphor. The discovery of the relevant new principle, together with the crucial experimental proof of that principle, is the reality which corresponds to that metaphor. So, in physical science, we give the name of the discoverers of the paradoxes and their solutions to the paradox and its solution, just as we give the name of a composer and of the relevant metaphor to a Classical-artistic composition.

In physical science, it is such experimental solutions to well-defined such paradoxes, which define *knowledge*, as distinct from mere learning. One knows a principle only if one has replicated the relevant paradox and its corresponding, discovered principle of solution. Knowledge is the accumulation of such replications of validated discoveries of principle. That is to emphasize, that knowledge lies in the succession of valid discoveries which have been mastered by the stu-

---

53. For Kepler's proof of the elliptical character of the Mars orbit, see Johannes Kepler, **New Astronomy,** trans. by W.H. Donahue (Cambridge, U.K.: Cambridge University Press, 1992). The proof is discussed in Jonathan Tennenbaum and Bruce Director, "How Gauss Determined the Orbit of Ceres," **Fidelio,** Summer 1998 (in press).

54. Cusa, *loc. cit.*

55. The proof of the transcendental character of $\pi$ is a perfect model of this kind of proof of existence of a necessary, new physical principle.

dent, for example; what one may have "learned" in other ways, does not constitute knowledge. Merely passing written and oral examinations, does not measure knowledge, but, usually, measures only the inferior mental condition of mere learning.

This is precisely parallel to the case we identified for Classical artistic composition. The composition does not lie in the details produced, but rather in the process of development which lies "outside" and above anything so produced. Just so, the paradoxes which force the audience to recognize the need for a higher principle of change, shift the location of the drama (for example) from the literal features of the composition, to the principle of ordering which underlies the succession of changes in state, those transformations of hypothesis, which is the unity of the entire composition.

To restate the crucial issue once again: Reality does not lie in a deductive form of representation of experiences as those phenomena are situated in terms of a fixed hypothesis. Reality lies in that higher authority which exists above any one hypothesis, which exists in the ordering of a valid succession of hypotheses. The reality experienced in that succession, is the "substance" of the experience of this succession. That is the crucial ontological issue of physical science; there lies the efficient interconnection between the ordering of realized scientific progress and the development of the principles of Classical culture.

At this point, on this account, a deeper problem confronts us.

The more thoroughly we attempt to exhaust the lessons of physical scientific progress as such, such as a Riemannian representation of such progress, the more stubbornly a certain perplexity confronts the scientific thinker. There are two leading issues. First, what is the nature of that creative process, by means of which the mind generates valid solutions of principle for crucial experimental-scientific paradoxes? Second, what is the active ordering-principle associated with such valid discoveries of principle? If we reflect carefully on what these considerations imply, we must recognize that there is no adequate formal-scientific answer for these two questions. This leads us to discover a second manifold, an m-fold manifold of principles of Classical-artistic composition. This m-fold manifold expresses the passion, the driving and directing force which underlies and otherwise governs both scientific and artistic progress.

## 4. Order in Physical Science

Since Plato's dialogues, the leading intellectual currents of European civilization have focussed upon the implications of a certain central paradox, a central metaphor, as the central issue of scientific principle respecting our universe taken as a whole. From the root supplied by Plato's emphasis upon a parallel between the characteristic of living processes and principles of musical composition, Plato, Luca Pacioli, Leonardo da Vinci, and Johannes Kepler, among others, have emphasized two qualitatively distinct kinds of ordering within the physical universe: those orderings cohering with the Golden Section, and those which do not. Living processes, in particular, cohere with the former, but, as Kepler emphasized, also ostensibly non-living systems, such as the Solar System as a whole. For our purposes, we associate non-living systems generally with entropic processes, and living ones as the most exactly paradigmatic expression of not-entropic processes in general.[56]

Perhaps the most efficient approach to conceptualizing those distinctions, is the case of the not-entropic physical-economic process. There is nothing to be properly viewed as accidental in this view of physical economy. The central practical question of all knowledge, is the question: Is man's knowledge of the physical universe, merely his conceit, or is there some objective proof, by means of which one kind of thinking corresponds, demonstrably, to the lawful ordering of our universe, and a contrary kind of thinking does not? In this matter, there ought to be no objection to the proposition, that the test of human knowledge is posed by the question: Does a certain method of transformation of human knowledge result, unquestionably, in a process of increase of mankind's mastery of the universe?

The general form of the answer to this question, appears at the moment, we shift the issue of mastery, from focus on the practice of the particular, isolated individual, to measuring the increase of the human species' power to increase its per-capita power over nature. This increase must be defined with the attached condition, that the potential relative population-density is also increased by this change. To express this connection in a rigorous way, we must introduce the

---

56. E.g., consider Vernadsky's notion of the noösphere.

notion of the progressive ordering of higher hypothesis and increase of mankind's potential relative population-density.

We are confronted, then, with two distinct, but interdependent aspects of the human species' increase of its potential relative population-density. One, is the relationship of the human species to the given biosphere within which it is presently, or recently located; the other, is the actions of mankind affecting the increase of potential of the biosphere to serve as a foundation for increase of mankind's potential relative population-density. The simplest way to force attention to these combined considerations, is to look at such challenges of the coming century as colonizing another planet, or even terra-forming it.

Ask ourselves: Given, the total set of preconditions, including the biosphere's current state of development, upon which we must depend for the per-capita and per-square-kilometer perpetuation of the total current output of our species. What must we produce, to maintain at least a continuous supply of that quality and quantity of consumption?

Situate the notion of potential relative population-density, per capita and per square kilometer, in respect to investment in maintaining and improving the output of our species, per capita and per square kilometer.

To this purpose, we must place emphasis upon the demographic characteristics of the population. Rate of growth of the population, is a consideration. Consider life-expectancy, examined for the cost of developing a new individual, as against the loss to society from high rates of infant mortality and lowered life-expectancy in general. For example, consider the quality of development of the physical-economic investment by the society in scientific and technological potential of the new individual as a desired improvement in the physical-economic demographic characteristics of the population.

Consider some elements of basic economic infrastructure: transport, water, and energy. To the extent we can slow down the rate at which water, originating as rainfall, is emptied into the seas and oceans: in how many ways can the useful turnover of that water-flow be increased? Can we increase, thus, the effective amount of water available per capita and per square kilometer? How can we better manage forests, fields, and so forth, to increase and effectively maintain water-tables, streams, and create weather-systems which moderate weather and increase the amount of rainfall regenerated from evaporation? How can we better develop water as a means of relatively low-cost transport, while also using the same water for other purposes? Similarly, how can we increase not only the raw energy supplies per capita and per square kilometer, but how might we also increase the effective energy-flux density deployed per capita and per square kilometer, for the benefits expressed in the environment generally, and in per-capita productivity?

As we increase the range of applied scientific principles and derived technologies, we increase the complexity of the division of labor. We also increase the level of education required to produce a population which has assimilated a relatively higher level of scientific and artistic principles. This requires an increase in the number of years, prior to biological maturity, devoted to education and related matters; that expenditure for education and Classical culture, is a part of the necessary cost of increasing and maintaining the potential productivity of the population, per capita.

For the simplest representation of the result, we divide the physical-economic output of society into three categories: Total useful output, cost of maintaining that magnitude and rate of total output, and the ratio of total output to total required inputs, the latter including the necessary maintenance and further development of basic economic infrastructure. To maintain a culture, is therefore expressed in the following general constraints. The technological level must be raised; total output per capita and per square kilometer, must increase; yet, the ratio of total output to total required inputs, must increase; meanwhile, the total required inputs, per capita and per square kilometer, must also increase. *This set of constraints typifies a not-entropic process.* This physical-economic "model" must be used to supply a competent, rigorous definition of the very terms "not entropic," or "anti-entropic."

The physical-economic condition under which that not-entropic requirement is satisfied, expresses the result of applying the creative-mental potential of the species to man's increasing power over nature. The creative process so realized as applied advances in knowledge, expresses the lawful composition of our universe. That is, the condition under which mankind's willful actions, to proceed from a previous to a higher quality of hypothesis, satisfy that not-entropic requirement, expresses the power of our species to command such obedience from the universe in general. *In other words, the universe as a whole is lawfully non-entropic.* In competent science, no "law of universal entropy" is tolerated.

Consider two additional implications of this physical-economic expression of "anti-entropy:" first, the form in which anti-entropy is expressed in terms of a Riemannian n-fold manifold of physical principles; second, a similar expression in Classical art-forms. The simpler case is the straight realization of an n- to (n+1)-fold progress in discovery of scientific principles as realized technological progress in the productive powers of labor. The second case, is that of increasing density of discovered and realized Classical-artistic principles. In both implications, anti-entropic action is of the form and content of $F[(n+1)/n]$, or, $F'[(m+1)/m]$. It is through this action upon the universe by the creative powers of the individual human mind, that human activity realizes anti-entropic growth, and related progress, in mankind's relationship to the universe at large.

Clearly, in addressing the notion of anti-entropy in a more general way than is required by the subject of culture as such, we could not overlook two other cases. First, obviously, we must take into account those characteristics of life as such, which lie entirely outside entropy, as these are expressed, for example, in the development of the biosphere even before the existence of the human species. Second, we must go further, as Plato, Pacioli, Leonardo, and Kepler did, to recognize that the same principle of anti-entropy underlies the deeper principles of ordering in the universe at large.

Pending that attention to these latter two, other expressions of anti-entropy, the crucial fact on which to focus here, is that human creativity occurs solely within the bounds of the individual mental-creative processes, and does not occur as a product of interaction among those individuals. That is to stress, that all evidence of that creative mentation which generates either a validated new physical principle, or comparable principle of Classical artistic development, occurs only within the individual mind. Such discoveries of principle can be spread in society, but only through replicating the original act of discovery, one mind at a time.

The special fact to be stressed here, is that Classical artistic creativity, as typified by Plato's notion of the *idea*, is the only case in which the creative powers of the individual mind are applied directly to those creative mental processes themselves. It is the study of the progressive development of those social processes associated with progress, in terms of Classical-humanist art-forms which, alone, provides the human mind access to comprehension of the potential of the individual's human creative processes themselves. Therein lies the manifestly superior position of Classical art-forms over all other forms of knowledge. The treatment of education from the standpoint of Schiller and of his friend Wilhelm von Humboldt, represents, thus, the highest expression of statecraft, the development of those young minds which must supply future progress in statecraft.

## 5. Education and the Tragic Principle

The essential issue of an individual's personal morality, is posed by the question, whether personal self-interest is located as the fascists such as Nazi existentialist philosopher Martin Heidegger did, in the pettiness of day-to-day and similarly small-minded personal and family responsibilities and gratifications, or, rather, in terms of the outcome one seeks for one's life, from birth to death, taken in the totality of that life's outcome for the past and future existence of the human species in general. This requirement must be read as a life conducted to supply an enhanced role for one's participation in one's culture, one's nation, a life lived as the instrument through which the universal outcomes of one's life are realized.

Restate and amplify that crucial issue of morality as follows. The essence of the individual's life, is the simple fact, that each among us is born and will die. On this account, the fundamental self-interest of each individual is located in the continuing outcome of that mortal life, an outcome which reverberates far beyond the time prior to one's birth, and after one's demise.

The corresponding peculiarity of that individual's self-interest, in absolute distinction from the nature of the beasts, is that our effect upon the importance of the individual for the human species as a whole, is located in the value for all mankind of those Platonic *ideas* which represent the accumulation of valid, discovered principles of the universe which we have assimilated from our forebears, and will thus, and otherwise transmit to our posterity. These ideas include not only the n-fold manifold of physical science, but also the m-fold manifold of cultural principles.

That view of ideas, is the basis upon which the thoughtful persons asks, "What is the outcome of my having lived? Is it, perhaps, the deeds I do, or the pain or pleasure which I experienced? Or, is it something less mortal, less perishable than mere deeds, mere acquisitions, mere pleasures?" What endured when Classical Greece died?

Plato endured.

What was enduring was the efficiency of those *ideas* corresponding to validatable discovery of principle. When we relive the valid discoveries of those who have gone before us, we perpetuate the good they have bequeathed to us, and we relive in ourselves that which is enduring, which they have given to us in this way. Thus, we, the bearers of the gifts of knowledge of *ideas* from past generations, may not only perpetuate the precious ideas passed down to us from earlier generations, even after the death of those ancients, but we may add something valid and new to that stock of principles to be transmitted to the benefit of the future. In such ways, we may impart living immortality to the gifts of the past, and become also a necessary part of that which follows the end of our mortal existence.

Persons who meet that standard, become *world-historical beings*. They never die, because that which is essential in their having lived, lives on as the benefit which ideas from the past have bequeathed to the future.

Consider the pupil from the elementary and secondary grades of education. Consider the pupil's education from the standpoint just summarized.

Is it important that the student learn in school? Or, is it *relatively* unimportant? Know, that learning is almost nothing; know that knowing is almost everything. The essence of morality in all education of the young, is the replication of the act of discovery of valid ideas. When the student has generated, or replicated the act of a validatable discovery of principle, he or she *knows* that principle, and is able to transmit it to others, not as mere learning, but, rather, as knowledge for practice. A moral educational institution, is one in which the pupils relive the experience of knowing valid principles, both those principles relived, as discovery, from the past, or added to the stock of such principles. That connection to *ideas*, rather than mere learning, locates all of us who follow the path of such ideas, both as students and adults, as a continuation of the history of ideas, as a person embodying the past in acting to create the future.

The order in which notions of principle are generated, is the procession of history. Only persons who locate their personal self-interest and identity in that kind of relationship to ideas, are world-historical individuals.

Consider again the difference between the definition of "morality" in the mouth of a bestialized existentialist, such as a follower of Nazi philosopher Martin Heidegger, or his depraved clone, Jean-Paul Sartre. The existentialist has merely learned; he, or she lacks that notion of morality natural to a world-historical individal. That existentialist, that follower of Thomas Hobbes, John Locke, or Immanuel Kant, has no true morality. It is the continuing outcome of my having once lived, which is the essence of the known self-interest of the world-historical individual. My pleasures, my pains, my losses, my gains, are as nothing compared to what I gain, or lose, in securing, or failing to serve the immortal meaning of my world-historical existence.

Situate Platonic ideas as existing, ontologically, within the domain of *higher hypothesis*. Reality is, thus, that process by means of which man's mind is transformed from relatively lower, to higher states, as from the state of a relatively valid n-fold manifold of physical science, to a higher one, (n+1)-fold. Or, in respect of moral principles, from m-fold, to (m+1)-fold. The process of change, in Heraclitus' and Plato's sense of *change*, is the location of the continuing substance of change, from relatively lower to higher states.

In this view, every person who meets the moral requirement of being, effectively, a world-historical individual, dwells in the eternity of change. In other words, in the brief time we live and act as world-historical individuals, we exist forever, in *the simultaneity of eternity*. So, each of us must be judged. So, each of us must judge himself or herself. So, our conscience is to be ruled in all matters of moment-to-moment behavior; so, our conscience must situate our notion of our primary self-interest, our interest as efficiently located within the simultaneity of eternity.

That view, which locates the fundamental self-interest of both the individual person, culture, and nation, as its world-historical self-interest, is the standpoint from which Classical tragedy is to be composed, performed, and assimilated; this is the standpoint of Aeschylos' **Prometheus Bound**, and the tragedies of Shakespeare and Schiller. What is the world-historical interest of a Prometheus, enduring immortal torment, that he might keep the secret, and thus ensure the self-induced doom of those common enemies of the Creator and mankind, the ruling oligarchy of satanic Zeus' Olympus? What is the world-historical duty which Hamlet, as Prince of endangered Denmark, must adopt, overriding all merely personal issues to the end of serving that duty? What were the world-historical duties variously shirked by Posa, Don Carlos, and King Philip? It is that world-historical view which must excite our passions to do good, to act as, and to be a world-historical person rooted in the simultaneity of eternity.

Consider a more general expression of the world-historical issues so defined.

Until the revolutionary changes introduced by the Fifteenth-Century Council of Florence, and by the ensuing reconstruction of France under King Louis XI, approximately ninety-five percent of mankind, in all cultures, lived in a condition of degradation to the status of virtual human cattle. The society within which these "human cattle" were herded, was a society ruled by an oligarchy. This oligarchy was composed of a blending of several types: a landed aristocracy, such as that of feudal Europe; a financier aristocracy, such as that of Venice or today's London; or an administrative oligarchy of the bureaucratic type. The definition of law under such oligarchies, was, predominantly, a privilege of the ruling oligarchy, an oligarchy which possessed the society and its people, as a feudal landlord of Dr. François Quesnay's evil type owned land, cattle, and serfs.

All forms of oligarchical society, including the principle of western feudal Europe, as of Byzantium, were, and are essentially evil. The essential evil in all forms of oligarchical society, is the denial of the individual's right to participate in the rule of society by the process of development of valid ideas. In other words, the essence of evil, is the crime of the very mere existence of satanic Zeus' Olympian oligarchy, or, Olympus' surrogate, the cult of Apollo (Apollo-Gaea-Python-Dionysus). The essence of evil is the denial of the right to be developed, and to become a world-historical individual, a participant in the simultaneity of eternity.

At this juncture, a crucial point must be interpolated. U.S. President Polk was an evil man, and his war against Mexico was a crime against the vital interests of the United States. On these matters, U.S. Representative (and later President) Abraham Lincoln was consistently right; but, on the larger issues of culture, Henry David Thoreau was a wicked man. There was no more evil doctrine ever concocted, than the myth of "the noble savage," or the related notion of the nobility of "the simple life."

Indeed, the role of the British agents, and agents of influence, Philippe Egalité, and the Jacobins Danton, Marat, Robespierre, Saint-Just, et al.,[57] exemplifies the evil which shocked such German apostles of liberty as Friedrich Schiller. The instrument which these sundry British agents and assets mustered to destroy France from within, was the rabble called into Paris for such enterprises as the storming of the Bastille, for Philippe Egalité's raid on Versailles, and the Jacobin Reign of Terror.

Although the philosophical basis for the overcoming of oligarchical society was supplied by Plato et al., the actual transformation was the cumulative result of Christianity, the ministries of Jesus Christ and the Apostles John and Paul most notably. The obvious root of the modern notion of freedom and equality, is the principle first established by Christianity, that all persons are equally made in the image of the Creator, with no preference to one or another national, cultural, or ethnic discrimination allowed. Notable, is the fact that this work of Christianity was undertaken within the scope of a Hellenistic Mediterranean culture which was derived from the Classical Greek of Plato and his influential Academy. The Apostles John and Paul made that cultural heritage of Plato the medium in which the Christian mission was continued. It was these Christian Platonic conceptions, typified by the role of the Augustinian tradition, which became the leading edge of the centuries-long struggle out of which the Fifteenth-Century Golden Renaissance emerged.

That struggle, typified by the work of Abelard of Paris, of Frederick II, of Dante Alighieri, of Petrarch, of teaching orders such as the Brothers of the Common Life, and so on, was a struggle to establish a form of society based upon the nation-state, rather than some oligarchical classes which placed themselves above accountability to the idea of a nation as belonging to its people, rather than some intrinsically oligarchical institution placed above the people. This idea of the nation-state republic had nothing to do with the perverted notions of "democracy" associated with John

---

57. Danton and Marat were both directly agents trained and deployed, from London, by the head of the British foreign service, Jeremy Bentham. Philippe Egalité was an agent of the pro-London faction, and was the organizer of that farce, known as the storming of the Bastille, which Philippe organized, armed, and led as an election-campaign stunt on behalf of the Swiss banker (and father of the the evil Madame de Staël), Jacques Necker, who had just earlier bankrupted France on behalf of London's strategic interest.

Locke, but rather, the accountability of the ruling institutions of society to the principle of universal truth and justice, the principle that all persons must have the right to develop and live as world-historical personalities.

There are two great evils predominating in the known existence of our species. One, is the evil of oligarchism, as typified by the administrative oligarchies of ancient Mesopotamia and Rome, the feudal aristocracy of Europe, and the financier oligarchy of such institutions as the Delphi cult of Apollo, Venice, and London today. The other great evil, is the moral degeneracy deeply imbued in those subject populations whose moral condition and impulses have been degraded, by oligarchical rule, into the relative bestiality of human cattle. The practical ordinary person may have the nobler impulses of the human individual, but, under oligarchical traditions, the circumstances of practical life cause that person to be self-dominated by relatively brutish, "practical" considerations. Therein lies that evil among the "ordinary people," by means of which, usually, oligarchy preserves its control over the popular will.

The great issue of culture, is the task of freeing the majority of the population from that moral and intellectual self-degradation which tradition imbues within prevailing popular opinion.

The issue of individual human freedom, is not the issue of "democracy," not democracy as the moral degenerates of today's National Endowment for Democracy misuse the term, not like degenerates such as John Dewey, nor as Nazi-like existentialists such as Schopenhauer, Nietzsche, Heidegger, and Jean-Paul Sartre generally define democracy. The issue is the right of every newborn child to be developed in a way which represents access to, and imposition of the rule of truth and justice, to ensure that quality of progress in the human condition which meets the need of the individual to be a world-historical personality, to be a resident of the simultaneity of eternity. This means the obligation of society to direct the shaping of the policies of practice of the society to bring about progress in such upward directions of individual world-historical participation in ideas.

The essential feature of persons who lack freedom, is their emulation of the condition of human cattle. They are conditioned to respond to what human cattle would consider the matters of personal self-interest, the motives of the "Seven Deadly Sins," the motive of my narrowly defined personal and family self-interests, and of society as a whole, either a poor second, or, like the typical existentialist, virtually not at all. It is their attachment to those baser motivations which constitutes the shackles upon the self-enslaved individual degraded to a moral condition like that of virtual human cattle. These are the motivations of the Ku Klux Klanner and similar Jacobin rabble. For such human cattle, the definition of "freedom to choose" is nothing other than those depravities by which they are self-enshackled into the moral condition of virtual human cattle. It is by such libertarian's moral self-debasement, pursued "in my personal interest," or, "my freedom to choose," that the popular masses usually choose the pathway to their own self-debasement and oligarchical enslavement.

It is these world-historical concerns which define morality and true Classical culture. It is those principles of culture, of social and political life, which correspond to advancement of the condition of the individual and society to higher states, to relatively more not-entropic states, which represent the m-fold manifold of culture. The relationship between the m-fold and n-fold manifolds, is that the social requirements of progress in the former respect must direct the practical requirements of the latter respect.

The essence of freedom, is the right to define oneself as a world-historical individual, rather than some self-debased libertarian fool.

The essential difference between the raw, half-educated human being, and what Schiller identifies as "the beautiful soul," is located in the kind of change in the adolescent personality (for example) accomplished by aid of the kind of Classical-humanist education upon which stress is placed here. The point at which the individual passes over from a raw, morally semi-literate brute, into a "beautiful soul," is the point at which the student (for example) makes a qualitative transition, from selfishness to the moral impulses of an efficiently conscious world-historical personality. It is at the point, that the moral imperative of judgment, of personal commitment, is located entirely in a sense of devotion to one's world-historical soul. That transformation in the individual's sense of personal, world-historical identity, is the proper object of education; that transformation represents the threshold at which the immature adolescent (of all ages) is superseded by spiritual metagenesis into emerging as a true, world-historical citizen of a republic.

# 6. Classical Composition

The general moral requirement which sets Classical forms of artistic culture apart from, and above all alternatives, is the urgency of freeing human beings from the degraded state describable as "symbol-mindedness."

In plastic art, for example, Leonardo da Vinci exemplifies the duality of all Classical art. This duality is expressed, on the one side, as the obligation to subordinate the composition of plastic art to scientific truthfulness. On the other side, truth demands that we recognize the ironies, the metaphors, to which we must be led by any truthful scrutiny of principles of composition. Leonardo's revolutionary view of the vanishing-point, is an example of this ironical principle.[58] The role of two sources of light in Leonardo's **Virgin of the Rocks**, is a model of such metaphor.[59] The fact that Raphael Sanzio's **The School of Athens**[60] and **Transfiguration** must be conceptualized as the integration of the ambiguity of two (lower versus higher) viewpoints, is another.[61]

These ambiguities oblige the mind to abandon the literalness of sense-certainty, to subsume contradictory impressions by a resolving metaphor resident within the domain of ideas. In other words, to abandon deceitful sense-certainty, and also the intellectual and moral degradation expressed by the symbolic, or, related, "mannerist" views of art, in favor of truth.

Take the exemplary case of the Acropolis. Studies show that the Acropolis is the result of the unfolding of a single, coherent plan, always subsumed by the Classical Greek notion of Golden-Section-pivotted beauty in plastic art.[62] In effect, the resulting construction has the quality of a single, if "polyphonic" act of composition.[63]

Now, shift the focus: to, first, the principle of Classical tragedy, next, science in its aspect as a moral principle of art, and, finally, the substance which subsumes the process of development of Classical motivic thorough-composition, from J.S. Bach's development of polyphony, through the elaboration which Haydn, Mozart, Beethoven, Schubert, Brahms, et al. developed on the basis of the always-polyphonic foundation supplied by the later composers' study of Bach's work.

In their entirety, the dialogues of Plato, are exemplary works of Classical art. When the Homeric epics and the related Classical Greek tragedies are taken as the standpoint of reference for the entire body of Plato's collection of dialogues, we are able to trace the modern tragedies of Shakespeare and Schiller from this route, and also situate, similarly, the role of Plato's and other Classical-Greek models in the late-Eighteenth- and early-Nineteenth-Century efforts to revive the Classical tradition in poetry and drama. The most fruitful standpoint from which to view this entire Classical tradition, from ancient Greece into the Nineteenth Century, is the standpoint of historian-poet-tragedian Schiller's intended audience, the audience transformed into better people leaving the theater than had entered it a few hours earlier.

The essential feature of the Classical tragedy, and poem, is to induce the members of the audience to situate themselves as world-historical figures, as persons provoked into viewing the Classical performance as the prompting of the viewing of the subject-matter from a world-historical standpoint. In other words, the member of the audience must adopt a sense of world-historical responsibility for the real-life issues addressed by the drama or poem: "Could such characters not see the nature and consequences of their folly, for their society in their time? Must we, in our time, not learn the lesson of this, that we, in our time, must address the issues specific to our historical setting as those should have done in the historic specificity of the time shown on stage?"

To this end, it is essential that a Classical tragedy never be dressed up in modern costume, or otherwise presented as a timeless fable equally appropriate to past or present times.

The essence of history is the history of ideas. History is a record of variously forward, backward, and sideways movements in the course of mankind's obligation to progress to the level of higher manifolds of both physical-scientific and moral practice. The sundry diverging and interwining branches of the sundry, for-

---

58. See D. Stephen Pepper, "Leonardo da Vinci, Founder of Modern Technology," **New Solidarity,** May 2, 1983, and Karel Vereycken, "The Invention of Perspective," **Fidelio,** Winter 1996.

59. Leonardo da Vinci, **The Virgin of the Rocks,** the Louvre Museum, Paris.

60. Raphael Sanzio, **The School of Athens,** Vatican Museum.

61. Raphael Sanzio, **The Transfiguration,** Vatican Museum.

62. On the Golden Section, see *Timaeus,* in **Plato: Vol. IX,** Loeb Classical Library (Cambridge, Mass.: Harvard University Press, 1975). The Loeb Classical Library translations have the advantage of including the Greek text on the facing page. See also, the translation commissioned by Lyndon LaRouche, "Plato's Timaeus: The Basis of Modern Science," **The Campaigner,** February 1980.

63. Pierre Beaudry, "The Acropolis of Athens: The Classical Idea of Beauty," **New Federalist,** June 24, 1988.

Wolfgang Amadeus Mozart at the keyboard. *"The entirety of the development of well-tempered, polyphonic forms of motivic thorough-composition, from Bach through Brahms, is a sequentially ordered process of successive developments of musical ideas."*

www.arttoday.com

schools, such as Alessandro Scarlatti, et al., on the musical development of pre-Nineteenth-Century northern-Germany and southern-Germany music. Without the direct influence of J.S. Bach upon Mozart, Beethoven, et al., from the early 1780s onward, the post-1781 works of Mozart, Haydn, Beethoven, et al. had not been possible.[64] The entirety of the development of well-tempered, polyphonic forms of motivic thorough-composition, from Bach through Brahms, is a sequentially ordered process of successive developments of musical ideas.

This process of development, in music, in Classical tragedy, in Classical plastic arts, has a metrical quality. There are sequences, if not always simple, linear ones, and there is also a sense of density. Both notions, of sequence and density, are to be compared with the notion of Riemannian and quasi-Riemannian notions of interacting m-fold and n-fold manifolds.

## The Case of Music

In our focussing upon the case of music, here, we emphasize the importance of situating the particular development and performance of Classical musical composition in some medium whose primary content is nothing but sequence and density. This signifies that we must define a specific quality of impassioned idea which parallels and underlies the development of the composition and performance of Classical polyphony. This medium of passion is not hearing as such, but rather an idea of composition, addressed to the medium of hearing, but an idea superimposed upon hearing.

ward, sideways, and degenerative developments, are the skein of history, the skein of reality. The essential problem of historiography, as Classical tragedy exemplifies this, is to develop and maintain a sense of historic specificity in respect to the evolving mental, moral, and physical condition of mankind.

This sense of historic specificity, is best conveyed by Schiller's work in his functioning as both historian and tragedian. Significant ideas, if they are true, are never mere fiction; they are matters of historically specific kinds of ideas as they are situated, as a matter of principle, with respect to specific historical problems. It is a keen sense of the actual history in which these ideas are situated, which enables an audience to adduce a truthful sense of the solution to the paradox presented by the Classical tragedy.

The same rule of historic specificity applies to the history, and prehistory of modern music. Without the influence of the Fifteenth-Century Florentine *bel canto* voice-training, the development of Classical well-tempered polyphony, by J.S. Bach, would not have been possible. Without the indirect influence of J.S. Bach, as through C.P.E. Bach, Haydn's pre-1782 contributions to musical development would not been possible. All of this is intermingled with the influences of the Italian

64. Baron Gottfried van Swieten's music seminars in Vienna, in which Mozart participated, met every Sunday afternoon to play and study the manuscripts of Bach and Handel. See Bernhard Paumgartner, **Mozart** (Zürich: Atlantis Verlag, 1945), pp. 300-308; Hermann Abert, **W.A. Mozart** (Wiesbaden: Breitkopf & Härtel, 1983), pp. 75-79 and 117-165; and David Shavin, "The Battle Mozart Won in America's War with Britain," **Executive Intelligence Review**, Sept. 6, 1991.

In music, certain things come naturally. Primarily, the human speaking-singing voice is naturally predisposed to what are termed "register shifts." Although there are additional means which may be developed for the purposes of Classical-poetical coloration and dynamical expression of the human singing voice, natural registration is the dominant feature underlying both polyphony in general and the well-tempered polyphony clearly defined, in exemplary fashion, by Bach's polyphonic works for both singing and instrumental voices combined.[65]

The Florentine *bel canto* demonstrates the register-shifts most effectively. The effect of *bel canto* development, respecting the ratio of effort to what is heard, demonstrates the unique agreement of the *bel canto* voice-training with the natural potentialities of the voice. Similarly, voices which perform at a *bel canto*-determined C=256 survive longer, and better, than those burned out prematurely by overwork at artificially elevated pitches at, or above A=440, for example.

Then, once the ranges of the register shifts of the respective species of singing voices are determined, the mere task of employing a relevant counterpoint for such polyphony defines a primary approximation of a *bel canto*-determined well-tempered scale. At that point, a further refinement is required. The mind hears the inversion of any interval (e.g., C-E-G heard as G-E-C), to such effect that a simple Lydian scale is derived as an inversion of a C-minor, F♯ pivotted scale. The effort to bring the intervals represented by the scale indicated by the inversion, with the scale which has been inverted, introduces a further degree of refinement of the well-tempering. Add, then, inversions heard across the polyphonic parts to the inversions generated within each part, and a further refinement is introduced. Never is a precise, algebraic frequency determined; the infinitesimal approximation is always a non-linear one.

In other words, if we continue polyphonic and related developmental considerations, there is no simply algebraic determination of a well-tempered scale, but rather a counterpoint-determined interval of *non-constant curvature*, just as Johannes Kepler's approach, and Plato's earlier, point in that direction.

Once we pass from the level of considerations posed by J.S. Bach's **A Musical Offering** and **The Art of the Fugue**, into the generalized use of Lydian intervals by Mozart in the manner epitomized by his K.475 (and,

later, Beethoven's Opus 111), the span of Classical musical development, from Mozart of 1782-1783 through Brahms's **Vier Ernste Gesänge**, is opened up for us as a process of motivic thorough-compositional development, a process of increasing density, in the sense of Riemannian series of the n-fold type. When we combine the apparent, formal considerations with the implications of a new mode of song composition, by Mozart, Beethoven, Schubert, Schumann, Brahms, with all of the resulting interpretive considerations bearing upon the training and use of the singing voice, all Classical musical composition opens up for us through this "Rosetta Stone"-like medium of Classical song.[66]

On this account, the musician must hear with two sets of ears. One is the ear of simple hearing; the other, the mind's ear, which locates the driving passion of a composition in its developmental processes of change, the latter the ear which, like Wilhelm Furtwängler's, sings "between the notes." In music, for Pablo Casals, as for Heraclitus and Plato, nothing is constant but change. It is that principle of change which is the ontological foundation of all Classical art. In music, that foundation is located in the developmental process of constant change, which is the mind's ear.

Thus, when we sing with Bach, Haydn, Mozart, Beethoven, Schubert, Schumann, Brahms, and so on, we are expressing the essence of that playful domain in which the ontological essence of all art, and all morality, are supplied the ontological medium best suited to their expression. On this account, all great Classical music is, in its own way, sacred music, the soul's yearning toward its rightful, beautiful place in the simultaneity of eternity, as Bach's great student, Ludwig van Beethoven, best understood this.

## Truth in Statecraft

At this moment, the world—including the United States itself—is securely embarked on a journey to Hell, and, although the helmsman, including the current President of the United States, might deplore the ruin reaching to engulf us all, that President, thus far, has shown no inclination to reject the course of action, in

---

65. See **A Manual on the Rudiments of Tuning and Registration,** op. cit., Chapter 2.

66. The exemplary case is the conflict between Goethe and Reichardt, on the one side, and Mozart, Beethoven, Schiller, and Schubert, on the opposing side. See **A Manual on the Rudiments of Tuning and Registration,** op. cit., pp. 202-203.

economic policy, which ensures the impending destruction of both the United States and civilization as a whole. Although the President deplores the injustice and other sufferings into which the current direction of policy is carrying us all, so far he is unwilling to reject any of those of his own current policies which contribute to ensuring the worst result.

Take the case of the modern-day Henry Morgan, British privateer George Soros. Soros is outstanding among those whose predatory role has ruined such nations as Russia, and all among the nations of Southeast Asia, and much of East and South Asia otherwise. Yet, as in the case of looted Croatia, or Russia, the U.S. government repeatedly defends the role of Soros and his kind in destroying these nations—such as Malaysia, Thailand, Indonesia, the Philippines, etc., and in fostering those lunatic policies of the IMF and others which ensure the homicidal ruin of most of those economies—including our own—which the U.S. government professes itself dedicated to defend.

How is such folly possible? How is it possible that a President manifestly inclined to deeds of good will, could act so stubbornly contrary to the vital interests of his own administration, his nation, and civilization as a whole?

Two interacting factors are among those prominently to be considered. One is the political pragmatism of a heavily besieged President. The second, leading, interacting factor, is the President's own laundry-list of chosen agenda items: globalization, democracy, "information economy," "achievements of the Golden Generation," etc. On this account, the prevailing, implicitly suicidal policy-shaping trend is, that the choice of certain policies as "our policies," becomes not merely a substitute for truth, but, in practice, its direct opposite.

For example, for the better part of thirty years, the U.S. physical economy has been contracting consistently at rates averaging in excess of two percent per year. Over most of that period, a formerly (1946-1966) prosperous agro-industrial economy, has been looted by financial parasites, transforming a prosperous economy into what is now threatening to explode, momentarily, as the greatest financial bubble-collapse in world history. During the recent quarter-century, the physical-economic income and output of the U.S. population, per capita, has been contracting. The number of jobs taken, per household, in a futile effort to maintain a falling income-rate, does not keep up with the rate at which average household income is contracting. Yet, the current administration speaks of the successes of this economy, praising the futility of increasing the number of jobs by methods which reduce the per-capita family income for all but the super-rich parasites of Wall Street and like precincts! What happened to the truth?

To make short of a long list of kindred clinical evidence, we have come into a time when "democracy" has become a synonym for a fanatical sort of lying. Whatever is perceived to be popular opinion, whether it is actually popular opinion, or not, becomes the adopted policy which governs practice, that in defiance of all truthful evidence, and contrary to all sane reason.

Down among the *hoi polloi*, this folly is expressed as: "I don't care what you say, I have a right to my personal opinion," even when the evidence is entirely contrary to that misguided opinion. Truth is no longer a standard for policy-shaping practice. Such is the condition of a society which has lost the moral fitness to survive, the condition of a democracy which no longer either deserves to survive, or will survive. Such democracy is the sure road to a hellish tyranny under a regime whose subjects will, for better or worse, do precisely as they are told.

The root of this loss of moral fitness to survive, is readily and accurately traced back to such plainly immoral creatures as Paolo Sarpi's Francis Bacon and Thomas Hobbes, to John Locke, Bernard Mandeville, David Hume, Adam Smith, Jeremy Bentham, Immanuel Kant, Karl Savigny, and John Stuart Mill. On the one side, public and private morality is divorced from science; on the other side, science is divorced from morality. In the meantime, popular morality itself is degraded to the level of Mandeville's followers among the Eighteenth-Century British Hell Fire Clubs, the level depicted by Hogarth, the level of Hell as depicted in the most famous triptych of Hieronymous Bosch. The essence of our self-destruction during the recent thirty-five years of our downhill slide, has been the growth of what passes today for "popular opinion" and "popular culture."

Where are the men and women fit to lead us out of this peril? Where are those who will lead in the pathway toward safety, the pathway toward rule by the principles of truth and justice, not "popular opinion"?

For appendix commissioned by Lyndon La-Rouche, see http://larouchepub.com/eiw/public/1998/eirv25n35-19980904/eirv25n35-19980904_026-103-case_of_classical_motivic_th.pdf

# Lyndon LaRouche on the Significance of Donald Trump's Victory

*Feb. 21—The San Francisco Review of Books recently published an interview of Lyndon LaRouche by Joseph Ford Cotto, in five parts, of which the following is a condensation.*

**Cotto:** People have said a great many things about Lyndon LaRouche over the years.

To be fair, he has shared more than a bit about his own views—and why not? At 94, he has a lifetime of experience in traversing the maze of politics, economics, science, and cultural pursuits that makes our world go 'round.

While LaRouche's claim to fame is principally of a fiscal nature—his LaRouche-Riemann Method is perhaps the most accurate economic forecasting model yet devised—the man has delved into so many different facets of the human experience that one can legitimately elevate him to polymath status.

Whether one should read his views on classical music or space technology, it is a wonder that a single fellow is capable of holding so much knowledge about such a diverse array of topics. Even in the case that his views are found to be disagreeable, it must be admitted that he knows his stuff.

The child of an independent-minded New England Quaker family who served in World War II, LaRouche was imbued with a deep sense of purpose from a young age. Having interviewed the man on several occasions and reviewed his biography, it seems clear to me that, for the immense complexity of his life's work, the overarching goal is raising the bar of civilization so as many people as possible enjoy a more-than-decent standard of living.

Of course, certain voices will point out that he ran into a financial snafu with the federal government, for which he did some jail time, or that the LaRouche organization is run with military-like efficiency—something starkly unusual for civilian politics.

I say that nobody is perfect. I also say that, given his age and multitude of life lessons, he should be deemed a living historical monument. Special emphasis is due the word 'living' as LaRouche's movement is arguably stronger than ever, thanks to the Internet, and the finely-tuned publishing empire he built ensures that his views will remain in circulation for quite awhile.

LaRouche spoke with me about several timely issues. Some of our conversation is included below.

Lyndon H. Larouche gave his answers on January 13, 2017.

**Cotto:** A few years ago, certain political forecasters claimed that the future of America's center-right belongs to libertarians. Since the 2012 presidential election, protectionism has surged in both major parties. Now, in the age of Trump, libertarianism's once-ascendant nature seems a distant memory. Would you say that right-libertarian politics have any serious potential under Trump?

**LaRouche:** The point is the support for Trump's coming Presidency, that is the key. Right wing libertarian politics *per se* is not important. It is Trump and his role which is important. It is a new, improved practice. Trump has promised to invest $1 trillion in urgently needed infrastructure and promised the implementation of a 21st Century Glass Steagall Act. If he implements his infrastructure promise he will need that reform to finance it.

**Cotto:** More than anything else, why are protectionist economics transforming the American conservative movement?

**LaRouche:** Trump! Trump's method. Trump's way of dealing with the people. Protection—the issue is to make the economy work with real measures, as I just mentioned. It is a buoying up on Trump's efforts. It is not that the Old Right are no longer important, but is the question of bringing together a more novel way, not doing the same old thing. Ronald Reagan conservatives would surely find something interesting in Donald Trump. Absolutely! We had a president who was taken out of action [the assassination attempt on Reagan—Editor] but he came back in. It was not a simple thing, because I was one of the victims of that thing. What was done to him was that. Reagan survived the attack on him. He had a long period, extended period, an inability to function, but he got back into that function and he tried to build up more and more what he had as his intent, and I had been one of the key figures of his administration.

But we're talking about Trump. Really we're talking about Trump on the basis that he is now the new leader for the United States. He has promised to build up the American economy again, and there are great precedents of American Presidents using the American System of Economy as it was developed by Alexander Hamilton, explicitly in contrast to the British System of Free Trade. That is the system that worked in the past, and it will work again. Now, what Trump has done by his success, here, is to build up the possibility of a revival of the U.S. economy.

**Cotto:** The social justice warrior left and the alt-right have found success in spreading their ideas via Internet memes. Memes, by their very definition, are simplistic and emotional in nature. Untold millions of Americans, presumably Millennials in large part, appear more influenced by memes than longer, more reasonable arguments. Has the Internet dumbed down the political acumen of our country's young adults?

**LaRouche:** Yes, but there is, of course, still the potential of reversing that trend. Human beings are human beings, and once they have hope for their future, they get inspired to improve. On the Internet making people more stupid, it doesn't work that way. It is not the Internet *per se*. The education system has moved away from real scientific discovery. Young people think that because they got something from the Internet they know something. The question is, we have now this new government. Is the new one going to be better than the old? Everything follows from that.

**Cotto:** In America, entertainment is no longer clearly separated from news. Talk radio hosts, bloggers, and even television personalities devote time to amusing their audiences and vilifying the 'other side'—delivering a cartoonish version of reality which leaves untold millions misinformed. Is the average American adult now less cognizant of the issues than he or she might have been, say, 40 years ago?

**LaRouche:** Not quite. It comes from a different way. They are reduced in their functioning to an inferior level, compared to the former, better operation. What has happened is you have the degeneration of the effectiveness of the whole system. The citizens become citizens as such in a real sense, which Trump can do obviously—that's the change, that's the point. Given the economic data of the state of the U.S. labor force, shorter life expectancies, drug addiction, suicide rates, unemployment—a real effort to increase the real productivity of labor will be required. And Trump will have trouble with this thing, as he doesn't know how to explain the argument. Trump himself will understand the argument, but many of the people who are involved with him, as on his economic team, will have to face up to and understand this.

**Cotto:** What do you anticipate the primary legacy of Trump's election will be, specifically as far as American conservatism is concerned?

**LaRouche:** It will be the revival of the traditional U.S. American System of Economics, which will now have a better chance of succeeding given that other nations are moving in the direction of those Principles, like with "Win-Win" cooperation with China and the Belt and Road Initiative, where over 70 nations are using American System principles.

**Cotto:** For the sake of our national interest, was Trump's victory preferable to a Hillary Clinton win?

**LaRouche:** Ha! There is no comparison. She is dumped. She is not anything, she is a dump.

**Cotto:** More than anything else, why do you think Trump managed to secure a victory that many seasoned political operatives deemed unlikely?

**LaRouche:** That is sort of an amusing question. The answer is that Trump is actually supporting a refreshed status for the economy. The Trump vote in the U.S. is one of many expressions of populations being fed up with being victims of the system of globalization, which made the poor poorer and destroyed the Middle Class. Trump gave expression to that sentiment.

**Cotto:** How large a role do you believe that Barack Obama's presidency played in driving late-deciding voters into Trump's column?

**LaRouche:** No. There was no connection in that sense. The point was, we dumped that. Obama was dumped, and just keep it that way. Trump was the good guy as opposed to the bad guy. It is not a mystery for me, something that I have to explain away. Trump moved in and he changed the course of history. He got the job that Obama lost. Trump will have to lead a successful renewal of the economy of the United States.

www.ingramcontent.com/pod-product-compliance
Lightning Source LLC
Chambersburg PA
CBHW081559280526
45788CB00011B/3518